LEVELS 1-5

MONTESSORI READING REMEDIATION PATHWAY

SUPPORTING EMERGENT READERS

FIRST EDITION

TEACHER'S MANUAL

Montessori For All

Written by Montessori For All
with contributions from
Sarah Scott Frank, Yolanda Romanelli,
Stacie Scheller, and Sara Cotner

A special thanks to
Amy Osborn, Victoria Grogan,
Abi Hart, and Erica Gannon

Layout and Design by Sebrina Parker

Printed in the United States of America
First Edition: August 2021

TABLE OF CONTENTS

Accelerated Montessori Reading Development Trajectory

Level	Phonological Awareness (ORAL)	Writing (Encoding) & Reading (Decoding) Work	
		Phonics Elements to Focus on	Sight Words / Puzzle Words
1 9-12 weeks	1. Identify a Rhyme 2. Isolate Beginning Sound 3. Isolate Final Sound 4. Isolate Medial Sound 5. Blend Phonemes 6. Segment Phonemes 7. Generate a Rhyme 8. Compound Words: Delete First Word 9. Compound Words: Delete Second Word 10. Delete Beginning Sound 11. Delete Final Sound	**LETTER SOUND + LETTER NAME, BEGINNING BLENDING VC and CVC WORDS WITH ALL SHORT VOWELS:** *(If children know letter sounds but not names, they can progress to the next level.)*	I, a, the, like, you, see
2 6 weeks		**BLENDING CVCC/CCVC/CCVCC WORDS WITH SHORT VOWELS + 2-syllable phonetic words:** double consonants ss, ff, ll, glued sounds am and an, adding s to make plural, ck	friend, no, has, to, or, is, go, we, she, my, oh, for, OK, her, me, little, be, he
3 6 weeks		**CONSONANT DIGRAPHS + BEGINNING VOWEL DIGRAPHS:** ch, sh, th, ee, oo as in book and oo as in moon	of, that, by, down, what, from, birthday, do, their, they, away, are, put, bear, puzzle, great, giving, said
4 6 weeks		**VOWEL DIGRAPHS:** silent E, ay, ie, oa, oy	was, keys, so, sleepy, there, where, walking, window, new, goes, out, who, would, break, many, idea, solve, each
5 6 weeks		**R CONTROLLED VOWELS + INFLECTIONAL ENDINGS ED + ING:** ar, or, ir, er, + inflectional endings -ed and -ing	treasure, other, each, which, them, use, many, some, come, long, been, number, people, first, find, who, two, more

Note about Teaching Sight Words

This sequence includes sight word instruction to set children up to successfully read meaningful texts.

Sometimes words that are included as "sight words" are actually decodable. However, if they appear in books before children have been introduced to the phonetic elements, we support children to memorize them.

When teaching sight words, we can still help children recognize the decodable parts. For example, with the word said, we can point out that the s says /s/ and the d says /d/. Then we can support them to memorize that the ai sounds like /e/ in the word said.

When teaching sight words that will eventually be decodable, it's okay to preview the rule for children. For example, with the word sleepy, you could say, "Y at the end of a word often sounds like /ee/."

READING REMEDIATION PATHWAY: PHONICS SCOPE & SEQUENCE

How to Use This Book

We designed the Reading Remediation Pathway to use with kindergarteners in Children's House or Lower Elementary (1st-3rd grade) who are below the typical window of development. This reading remediation pathway uses Montessori methods (e.g., writing before reading) and Montessori materials (e.g., sandpaper letters, moveable alphabet, phonetic reading cards, etc.) to accelerate children's learning and help them get to a reading level of DRA 8 by the end of kindergarten (even if they start the year with no letter sounds) or to grow 1.5 years in 1st-3rd grades in a single academic year.

Step 1

Use the Montessori Phonics Screener to determine which level a child should start on. There are 9 levels. Once they pass all 9 levels, we switch to assessing them using the Reading A-Z running record assessment system and assign them a Fountas & Pinnell level instead of a phonics screener number

Step 2

Plan sufficient lessons for each child that is in Level 1-9. Lessons ideally happen one-on-one, especially in Levels 1-5. If that can't fit, you can meet with a small group at the same time. However, you will want to make sure that they are truly completing the activities independently. It is not helpful if they are copying their neighbor's work.

- *Children's House* = at least four lessons/week
- *Lower Elementary* = at least three lessons/week

Step 3

Build a system for keeping track of:
- which phonological awareness skills they have already mastered versus what they still need to work on.
- which sight words they have mastered.
- which phonetic elements they are working on and have already mastered.

A best practice for tracking sight words is to make a blank booklet for each child, write all the words on the back cover, use flashcards to teach sight words with a 3-period lesson, and write each word in the booklet as they master them. That way, the child can review previous sight words by reading their book to you at the start of each lesson.

You can also do this with the phonograms. As they master a phonogram, you can write the phonogram on a page and write ~5 words that have the phonogram in them. Be sure to write the phonogram in red pencil or ink.

Step 4

Start giving lessons! You can follow the guidance on the following page to structure your days:

Note about Materials

This Scope & Sequence is built around several different reading texts that have been carefully curated such that they are decodable in a scaffolded way (i.e., as children learn new phonetic elements or sight words, those elements start to appear in the texts). You can find a comprehensive list of texts needed for the Montessori Reading Remediation Pathway here: https://bit.ly/readingpathwaybooks

Sample Schedule

Day 1 Building and Blending	Day 2 Composing	Day 3 Reading	Day 4 (Children's House Only)
1. Practice phonological awareness (use appendix) 2. Read phonogram booklet: child reads previously mastered phonograms (STARTS LEVEL 2) 3. Read sight word booklet (STARTS WEEK 6 OF LEVEL 1) 4. Teach new sight words: use a 3-period lesson 5. Direct teach of the Lesson of the Week 6. Adult models how to build the first word (STARTS WEEK 2 OF LEVEL 1) 7. Guide dictates the remaining words for the child to build	1. Practice phonological awareness (use appendix) 2. Read phonogram booklet: child reads previously mastered phonograms (STARTS LEVEL 2) 3. Read sight word booklet (STARTS WEEK 6 OF LEVEL 1) 4. Teach new sight words: use a 3-period lesson 5. Review Lesson of the Week 6. Ask the child to build the phrases or sentences (If the child was not successful with word building on Day 1, repeat Day 1 before moving on)	1. Practice phonological awareness (use appendix) 2. Read phonogram booklet: child reads previously mastered phonograms (STARTS LEVEL 2) 3. Read sight word booklet (STARTS WEEK 6 OF LEVEL 1) 4. Teach new sight words: use a 3-period lesson 5. Review Lesson of the Week 6. Ask the child to read to you. Include time for a Comprehension Conversation.	1. Practice phonological awareness (use appendix) 2. Read phonogram booklet: child reads previously mastered phonograms (STARTS LEVEL 2) 3. Read sight word booklet (STARTS WEEK 6 OF LEVEL 1) 4. Teach new sight words: use a 3-period lesson 5. Review Lesson of the Week 6. Use the extra day to ensure that children are creatively composing text with the movable alphabet.

Day 1	Day 2	Day 3	Day 4
Phonological Awareness Practice			
Phonogram Review (of previously mastered words)			
Sight Word Review (of previously mastered words)			
Sight Word 3-Period Lesson (to teach new words)			
Guide directly teaches the sound of the week	Guide reviews the sound of the week		
Guide models how to build the first word	Ask the child to build the phrases or sentences	Ask the child to read to you and **ASK COMPREHENSION QUESTIONS**	Ask the child to compose a story using the Moveable Alphabet
Child builds remaining words			

LEVEL 1

LETTER SOUND/ LETTER NAME

Focus on beginning blending VC and CVC words with all short vowels

Level	Phonological Awareness (ORAL)	Writing (Encoding) & Reading (Decoding) Work	
		Phonics Elements to Focus on	Sight Words / Puzzle Words
1 9-12 weeks	1. Identify a Rhyme 2. Isolate Beginning Sound 3. Isolate Final Sound 4. Isolate Medial Sound 5. Blend Phonemes 6. Segment Phonemes 7. Generate a Rhyme 8. Compound Words: Delete First Word 9. Compound Words: Delete Second Word 10. Delete Beginning Sound 11. Delete Final Sound	LETTER SOUND + LETTER NAME, BEGINNING BLENDING VC and CVC WORDS WITH ALL SHORT VOWELS: *(If children know letter sounds but not names, they can progress to the next level.)*	I, a, the, like, you, see

LETTER SOUNDS/LETTER NAMES, FOCUS ON BEGINNING BLENDING VC AND CVC WORDS WITH ALL SHORT VOWELS

LEVEL 1 WEEK 1

DAILY PRACTICE

- Phonological Awareness Practice
- Review previously mastered letters
- 3-period lesson of letter sounds/names

    s   i   t

DAY 1

- Daily practice
- If children already know one or more of these letters, move on to the Week 2 letters. Use copy paper to make a small booklet for each child. As they master a new letter, add it to their book. You can use it to review the letter names and sounds that they have previously mastered at the start of each day.

DAY 2

- Daily practice

DAY 3

- Daily practice

DAY 4
(CHILDREN'S HOUSE ONLY)

- Daily practice

LETTER SOUNDS/LETTER NAMES, FOCUS ON BEGINNING BLENDING VC AND CVC WORDS WITH ALL SHORT VOWELS

DAILY PRACTICE

- Phonological Awareness Practice
- Letter Name & Sound Review
- 3-period lesson of letter sounds/names

    m   a   c

DAY 1

- Daily practice
- Dictate these words to children and have them build with the Movable Alphabet:
  it - sit - tim

DAY 2

- Daily practice
- Dictate these words to children and have them build with the Movable Alphabet:
  at - cat - mat

DAY 3

- Daily practice
- Dictate these words to children and have them build with the Movable Alphabet:
  at - cat - mat

DAY 4
(CHILDREN'S HOUSE ONLY)

- Daily practice
- Dictate these words to children and have them build with the Movable Alphabet:
  at - mat - sit - sat - cat

LETTER SOUNDS/LETTER NAMES, FOCUS ON BEGINNING BLENDING VC AND CVC WORDS WITH ALL SHORT VOWELS

DAILY PRACTICE

- Phonological Awareness Practice
- Letter Name & Sound Review
- 3-period lesson of letter sounds/names

  l   o   r

DAY 1

- Daily practice
- Dictate these words to children and have them build with the Movable Alphabet:
  lit - sit - sat

DAY 2

- Daily practice
- Dictate these words to children and have them build with the Movable Alphabet:
  lot - tom - cot

DAY 3

- Daily practice
- Dictate these words to children and have them build with the Movable Alphabet:
  rat - rot - rim

DAY 4
(CHILDREN'S HOUSE ONLY)

- Daily practice
- Dictate these words to children and have them build with the Movable Alphabet:
  rot - lit - cot - lot - rim - rat

LETTER SOUNDS/LETTER NAMES, FOCUS ON BEGINNING BLENDING VC AND CVC WORDS WITH ALL SHORT VOWELS

DAILY PRACTICE

- Phonological Awareness Practice
- Letter Name & Sound Review
- 3-period lesson of letter sounds/names
      b   e   n

DAY 1

- Daily practice
- Dictate these words to children and have them build with the Movable Alphabet: rob - mob - lob - bit - bat

DAY 2

- Daily practice
- Dictate these words to children and have them build with the Movable Alphabet: ten - set - bet - met - let

DAY 3

- Daily practice
- Dictate these words to children and have them build with the Movable Alphabet: ben - net - men- ten - not

DAY 4
(CHILDREN'S HOUSE ONLY)

- Daily practice
- Dictate these words to children and have them build with the Movable Alphabet: bet - set - met - bin - ten

LETTER SOUNDS/LETTER NAMES, FOCUS ON BEGINNING BLENDING VC AND CVC WORDS WITH ALL SHORT VOWELS

DAILY PRACTICE

- Phonological Awareness Practice
- Letter Name & Sound Review
- 3-period lesson of letter sounds/names

  h   u   g

DAY 1

- Daily practice
- Dictate these words to children and have them build with the Movable Alphabet: him - hit - hat - hen

DAY 2

- Daily practice
- Dictate these words to children and have them build with the Movable Alphabet: hum - cub - rub - sun - run

DAY 3

- Daily practice
- Dictate these words to children and have them build with the Movable Alphabet: hug - bug - rug - mug - sag

DAY 4 (CHILDREN'S HOUSE ONLY)

- Daily practice
- Dictate these words to children and have them build with the Movable Alphabet: hug - rug - big - hen - nut - bag

LETTER SOUNDS/LETTER NAMES, FOCUS ON BEGINNING BLENDING VC AND CVC WORDS WITH ALL SHORT VOWELS

LEVEL 1 WEEK 6

DAILY PRACTICE

- Phonological Awareness Practice
- Letter Name & Sound Review
- Teach new sight words
- 3-period lesson of letter sounds/names

    d   f   k   q   u

SIGHT WORDS OF THE WEEK

I, a, the

READING PRACTICE FOR THE WEEK:

bug

mug

fig

nut

bag

kit

dig

DAY 1

- Daily practice
- Dictate these words to children and have them build with the Movable Alphabet:
  dig - den - mud - sad - mad - rod

DAY 2

- Daily practice
- Dictate these words to children and have them build with the Movable Alphabet:
  fun - fin - fat - fig

DAY 3

- Daily practice
- Dictate these words to children and have them build with the Movable Alphabet:
  kit - kin - napkin

DAY 4 (CHILDREN'S HOUSE ONLY)

- Daily Practice
- Ask children to read the Reading Practice for the Week

LETTER SOUNDS/LETTER NAMES, FOCUS ON BEGINNING BLENDING VC AND CVC WORDS WITH ALL SHORT VOWELS

LEVEL 1 WEEK 7

DAILY PRACTICE

- Phonological Awareness Practice
- Letter Name & Sound Review
- Review new sight words
- 3-period lesson of letter sounds/names

  j   p   v

SIGHT WORDS OF THE WEEK
I, a, the

READING PRACTICE FOR THE WEEK:

pug

jug

jig

pen

pat

nap

DAY 1

- Daily practice
- Dictate these words to children and have them build with the Movable Alphabet: job - jut - jig

DAY 2

- Daily practice
- Dictate these words to children and have them build with the Movable Alphabet: pad - the pig - a pan - hip - pug

DAY 3

- Daily practice
- Dictate these words to children and have them build with the Movable Alphabet: the pug - a jug - the pen - best - slim

DAY 4
(CHILDREN'S HOUSE ONLY)

- Daily Practice
- Ask children to read the Reading Practice for the Week

LETTER SOUNDS/LETTER NAMES, FOCUS ON BEGINNING BLENDING VC AND CVC WORDS WITH ALL SHORT VOWELS

LEVEL 1 WEEK 8

DAILY PRACTICE

- Phonological Awareness Practice
- Letter Name & Sound Review
- Teach new sight words
- 3-period lesson of letter sounds/names

    y   w   x   z

SIGHT WORDS OF THE WEEK

like, you, see

READING PRACTICE FOR THE WEEK:

zit

zig

wet

wax

a fox

the box

DAY 1

- Daily practice
- Dictate these words to children and have them build with the Movable Alphabet:
  yet - yes - bit - let - rub

DAY 2

- Daily practice
- Dictate these words to children and have them build with the Movable Alphabet:
  wet - wig - wag - web

DAY 3

- Daily practice
- Dictate these words to children and have them build with the Movable Alphabet:
  the fox - the box - the vet - the six cats

DAY 4
(CHILDREN'S HOUSE ONLY)

- Daily Practice
- Ask children to read the Reading Practice for the Week

LETTER SOUNDS/LETTER NAMES, FOCUS ON BEGINNING BLENDING VC AND CVC WORDS WITH ALL SHORT VOWELS

LESSON OF THE WEEK

glued sound an

Explicit teaching: When a and n are right next to each other, they say /an/. Like ran. I ran to the park.

Start a Phonogram Word Review book for this child by writing an at the top of the page in red with ~5 an words (can, ran, hand, stand, fan). Use red for the -an in each word.

DAILY PRACTICE

- Phonological Awareness Practice
- Letter Name & Sound Review
- Review new sight words

SIGHT WORDS OF THE WEEK

like, you, see

READING PRACTICE FOR THE WEEK:

I like the plan.

I see the big man.

You see a tan can and fan.

DAY 1

- Daily practice
- Teach: 'an' sound
- Dictate these words to children and have them build with the Movable Alphabet: man - pan - ran - fan - and - ban

DAY 2

- Daily practice
- Review Lesson of the Week
- Dictate these words to children and have them build with the Movable Alphabet: tan - plan - can - hand - stand

DAY 3

- Daily practice
- Review Lesson of the Week
- Dictate these sentences to children and have them build with the Movable Alphabet:
  - I like the plan.
  - You see a tan fan and can.

DAY 4 (CHILDREN'S HOUSE ONLY)

- Daily Practice
- Review Lesson of the Week
- Ask children to read the Reading Practice for the Week

LETTER SOUNDS/LETTER NAMES, FOCUS ON BEGINNING BLENDING VC AND CVC WORDS WITH ALL SHORT VOWELS

LEVEL 1 WEEK 10

DAILY PRACTICE

- Phonological Awareness Practice
- Letter Name & Sound Review
- Sight word review

DAY 1

- Daily practice
- Dictate these words to children and have them build with the Movable Alphabet:
  set - nap - cub - hit - rod

DAY 2

- Daily practice
- Dictate these words to children and have them build with the Movable Alphabet:
  I like the red bug.
  I see a big rod.

READING PRACTICE FOR THE WEEK:

bet

trip

cup

sod

plan

DAY 3

- Daily practice
- Have child read:
  I like the big bug.
  (Ask: Can you imagine seeing a big bug?)
  Did you see the red rod?

DAY 4
(CHILDREN'S HOUSE ONLY)

- Daily Practice
- Ask children to read the Reading Practice for the Week

LETTER SOUNDS/LETTER NAMES, FOCUS ON BEGINNING BLENDING VC AND CVC WORDS WITH ALL SHORT VOWELS

DAILY PRACTICE

- Phonological Awareness Practice
- Letter Name & Sound Review
- Sight word review

READING PRACTICE FOR THE WEEK:

flap

plot

yet

flip

cut

DAY 1

- Daily practice
- Dictate these words to children and have them build with the Movable Alphabet:
  jet - lap - slug - bit - pop

DAY 2

- Daily practice
- Dictate these words to children and have them build with the Movable Alphabet:
  - Did you see the jet?
  - You can pop it.

DAY 3

- Daily practice
- Have child read:
  The jet is big and red.
  (Ask: Can you see that in your mind?)
  I did not pop it.
  (Ask: What is something that could pop that they might be talking about?

DAY 4 (CHILDREN'S HOUSE ONLY)

- Daily Practice
- Ask children to read the Reading Practice for the Week

LEVEL 2

BLENDS AND GLUED SOUNDS WITH SHORT VOWELS + 2-SYLLABLE PHONETIC WORDS

glued sounds am, -all, -ng; double consonants ss, ff, ll; ck; and s as z

SIGHT WORDS

friend, no, has, to, or, is, go, we, she, my, oh, for, OK, her, me, little, be, he

Level	Phonological Awareness (ORAL)	Writing (Encoding) & Reading (Decoding) Work	
		Phonics Elements to Focus on	Sight Words / Puzzle Words
2 6 weeks	1. Identify a Rhyme 2. Isolate Beginning Sound 3. Isolate Final Sound 4. Isolate Medial Sound 5. Blend Phonemes 6. Segment Phonemes 7. Generate a Rhyme 8. Compound Words: Delete First Word 9. Compound Words: Delete Second Word 10. Delete Beginning Sound 11. Delete Final Sound	**BLENDING CVCC/CCVC/CCVCC WORDS WITH SHORT VOWELS + 2-syllable** phonetic words: double consonants ss, ff, ll, glued sounds am and an, adding s to make plural, ck	friend, no, has, to, or, is, go, we, she, my, oh, for, OK, her, me, little, be, he

BLENDS AND GLUED SOUNDS WITH SHORT VOWELS + 2-SYLLABLE PHONETIC WORDS

glued sounds am, -all, -ng; double consonants ss, ff, ll; ck; and s as z

LESSON OF THE WEEK

glued sound am
Explicit teaching: When a and m are right next to each other, they say /am/. Like jam. I like to put jam on my toast.

DAILY PRACTICE

- Practice phonological awareness
- Read phonogram booklet
- Read sight word booklet
- Teach new sight words

SIGHT WORDS OF THE WEEK

friend, no, has

SENTENCES OF THE WEEK:

I clap.

Cam and Sam sat.

Do you like the dress?

DAY 1

- Daily practice
- Teach lesson of the week
- Dictate words:
  am, Sam, Cam, bam, clam, cram, slam
- Word build:
  am - Sam - Cam - bam - jam

DAY 2

- Daily practice
- Review lesson of the week
- Dictate sentences of the week

DAY 3

- Daily practice
- Ask child to read Sentences of the Week
- Ask child to read: I Am Sam (Emergent Reader Book 1)
- Engage in a comprehension conversation:
  - Who is Sam?

DAY 4
(CHILDREN'S HOUSE ONLY)

- Daily Practice
- Ask child to compose with the Movable Alphabet

BLENDS AND GLUED SOUNDS WITH SHORT VOWELS + 2-SYLLABLE PHONETIC WORDS

glued sounds am, -all, -ng; double consonants ss, ff, ll; ck; and s as z

LESSON OF THE WEEK

glued sound -all

When we put a-l-l together, it makes a special sound /all/. There are a lot of words that rhyme with all because they all end in a-l-l. Tall, fall. Can you think of any?

When you write your words today, be sure to use two l's.

DAILY PRACTICE

- Practice phonological awareness
- Read phonogram booklet
- Read sight word booklet
- Teach new sight words

SIGHT WORDS OF THE WEEK

to, or, is,

SENTENCES OF THE WEEK:

She sees the flock.

We will go to the track.

DAY 1

- Daily practice
- Teach lesson of the week
- Dictate words:
  all, ball, stall, wall, hall, mallet
- Word build:
  all - tall - ball - bill - will - hill

DAY 2

- Daily practice
- Review lesson of the week
- Dictate sentences of the week

DAY 3

- Daily practice
- Ask child to read Sentences of the Week
- Ask child to read: Can You See 3? (Emergent Reader Book 5)
- Engage in a comprehension conversation:
  - What are some of the things that the raccoon sees in the story?

DAY 4 (CHILDREN'S HOUSE ONLY)

- Daily Practice
- Ask child to compose with the Movable Alphabet

BLENDS AND GLUED SOUNDS WITH SHORT VOWELS + 2-SYLLABLE PHONETIC WORDS

glued sounds am, -all, -ng; double consonants ss, ff, ll; ck; and s as z

LESSON OF THE WEEK

glued sound -ng

When n and g go together they make a special sound like this: ring, thing, sing. Can you hear how it sounds like the sound is up in your nose?

DAY 1

- Daily practice
- Teach lesson of the week
- Dictate words:
  ring, sing, sang, rang, fang

DAY 2

- Daily practice
- Review lesson of the week
- Dictate sentences of the week

DAILY PRACTICE

- Practice phonological awareness
- Read phonogram booklet
- Read sight word booklet
- Teach new sight words

SIGHT WORDS OF THE WEEK

go, we, she

DAY 3

- Daily practice
- Ask child to read Sentences of the Week
- Ask child to read: Can I See Tom? (Flyleaf Emergent Reader 7)
- Engage in a comprehension conversation:
  - Who is the little girl searching for?
  - What are some of the things that she finds during her search?

SENTENCES OF THE WEEK:

The dog has fangs.

Did you sing the songs?

DAY 4
(CHILDREN'S HOUSE ONLY)

- Daily Practice
- Ask child to compose with the Movable Alphabet

BLENDS AND GLUED SOUNDS WITH SHORT VOWELS + 2-SYLLABLE PHONETIC WORDS

glued sounds am, -all, -ng; double consonants ss, ff, ll; ck; and s as z

LESSON OF THE WEEK

glued sound -all
double letters: -ff, -ll, and -ss

At the end of one-syllable words, we often double the letters f, l, and s when they come right after a single vowel.
These double letters just make one sound. So "dress" has two s's but it sounds like one. Or "fall" has two l's but sounds like one.

DAILY PRACTICE

- Practice phonological awareness
- Read phonogram booklet
- Read sight word booklet
- Teach new sight words

SIGHT WORDS OF THE WEEK

my, oh, for

SENTENCES OF THE WEEK:

We sit on the grass.

I miss my mom.

Get off the cliff.

DAY 1

- Daily practice
- Teach lesson of the week
- Dictate words:
  floss, hiss, less, pass, possum, gossip, muffin
  When you ask children to build 2- or 3-syllable words, model for them how to clap out each syllable (or say the word with their mouths closed if clapping doesn't work) and spell the word one syllable at a time.
- Word build:
  kiss - miss - moss - mess - less

DAY 2

- Daily practice
- Review lesson of the week
- Dictate sentences of the week

DAY 3

- Daily practice
- Ask child to read Sentences of the Week
- Ask child to read: Ms. Rhonda's Readers: The Pond
- Engage in a comprehension conversation:
  - Why does the pond change from being still to being not still?

DAY 4
(CHILDREN'S HOUSE ONLY)

- Daily Practice
- Ask child to compose with the Movable Alphabet

BLENDS AND GLUED SOUNDS WITH SHORT VOWELS + 2-SYLLABLE PHONETIC WORDS

glued sounds am, -all, -ng; double consonants ss, ff, ll; ck; and s as z

LEVEL 2 WEEK 5

LESSON OF THE WEEK

ck introduction

Explicit teaching:

When you hear a /k/ sound at the end of a word after a short vowel, it is often spelled with two letters: c and k. It can help to remember that both letters make a /k/ sound on their own, and they make a /k/ sound when they are together.

Examples of when to use -ck:

ă sack, pack

ĕ deck, fleck

ĭ sick, click

ŏ sock, lock

ŭ duck, luck

DAILY PRACTICE

- Practice phonological awareness
- Read phonogram booklet
- Read sight word booklet
- Teach new sight words

SIGHT WORDS OF THE WEEK

OK, her, me

SENTENCES OF THE WEEK:

No ducks can peck or cluck.

The dog runs to the stick.

DAY 1

- Daily practice
- Teach lesson of the week
- Dictate words:
  sock, pick, luck, crack, click, slack, truck, bucket, crickets
- Word build:
  duck - puck - pick - peck - neck

DAY 2

- Daily practice
- Review lesson of the week
- Dictate sentences of the week

DAY 3

- Daily practice
- Ask child to read Sentences of the Week
- Ask child to read: Ms Rhonda's Readers: Dog Day *(Introduce Woof! Woof! words as these are not decodable and oo has not been introduced)*
- Engage in a comprehension conversation:
  - What does the author mean when she writes "The dog has no friends?"
  - Why is the dog wagging and jumping in the middle of the story?
  - How do you think the dog feels at the end of the story?

DAY 4
(CHILDREN'S HOUSE ONLY)

- Daily Practice
- Ask child to compose with the Movable Alphabet

BLENDS AND GLUED SOUNDS WITH SHORT VOWELS + 2-SYLLABLE PHONETIC WORDS

glued sounds am, -all, -ng; double consonants ss, ff, ll; ck; and s as z

LEVEL 2 WEEK 6

LESSON OF THE WEEK

s as a z sound

Explicit teaching: There are two reasons we add -s to the end of a word. We add -s to show that there is more than one. So 1 pig. Two pigs. We can also add it to the end of verbs, which are action verb. So I run. Or she runs. Sometimes it sounds like /s/. Sometimes it sounds like /z/.

DAILY PRACTICE

- Practice phonological awareness
- Read phonogram booklet
- Read sight word booklet
- Teach new sight words

SIGHT WORDS OF THE WEEK

little, be, he

SENTENCES OF THE WEEK:

I can see the sleds.

I trip on the basket.

DAY 1

- Daily practice
- Teach lesson of the week
- Dictate words:
  pigs, hugs, pets, cots, baskets, cabinets runs, swims
- Word builds:
  dog - dogs - hogs - hog - hug - hugs

DAY 2

- Daily practice
- Review lesson of the week
- Dictate sentences of the week

DAY 3

- Daily practice
- Ask child to read Sentences of the Week
- Ask child to read: Cam and Sam (Emergent Reader Book 2)
- Engage in a comprehension conversation:
  - Do Cam and Sam like each other? How do you know?

DAY 4 (CHILDREN'S HOUSE ONLY)

- Daily Practice
- Ask child to compose with the Movable Alphabet

LEVEL 3

CONSONANT DIGRAPHS + BEGINNING VOWEL DIGRAPHS

ch, sh, th, ee, oo as in book and oo as in moon

	SIGHT WORDS
	of, that, by, down, what, from, birthday, do, their, they, away, are, put, bear, puzzle, great, giving, said

Level	Phonological Awareness (ORAL)	Writing (Encoding) & Reading (Decoding) Work	
		Phonics Elements to Focus on	Sight Words / Puzzle Words
3 6 weeks	1. Identify a Rhyme 2. Isolate Beginning Sound 3. Isolate Final Sound 4. Isolate Medial Sound 5. Blend Phonemes 6. Segment Phonemes 7. Generate a Rhyme 8. Compound Words: Delete First Word 9. Compound Words: Delete Second Word 10. Delete Beginning Sound 11. Delete Final Sound	**CONSONANT DIGRAPHS + BEGINNING VOWEL DIGRAPHS:** ch, sh, th, ee, oo as in book and oo as in moon	of, that, by, down, what, from, birthday, do, their, they, away, are, put, bear, puzzle, great, giving, said

CONSONANT DIGRAPHS + BEGINNING VOWEL DIGRAPHS

ch, sh, th, ee, oo as in book and oo as in moon

LESSON OF THE WEEK

ch

Explicit teaching: Sometimes two letters make one sound. *C-H is two letters but one sound, /ch/*

What words can you think of that begin with the CH sound

chop, cheese, cheer, chat, chew, champ, cheek, chair

What words can you think of that end with the CH sound: beach, bench, ouch, pouch, peach

---

DAILY PRACTICE

- Practice phonological awareness
- Read phonogram booklet
- Read sight word booklet
- Teach new sight words

SIGHT WORDS OF THE WEEK

of, that, by

SENTENCES OF THE WEEK:

Chop the tag off.

Her chips can be for lunch.

DAY 1

- Daily practice
- Teach lesson of the week
- Dictate words:
  chap, chops, chin, bench, lunch, checkup
- Word build:
  chap - chop - chops - hops - tops - stops

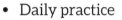

DAY 2

- Daily practice
- Review lesson of the week
- Dictate sentences of the week

DAY 3

- Daily practice
- Ask child to read Sentences of the Week
- Ask child to read: We Can't Stop (Emergent Reader Book 8)
- Engage in a comprehension conversation:
  - Where does the cop tell the cats to go?
  - What do they use to help them get to the top?
  - What happened at the top?

DAY 4
(CHILDREN'S HOUSE ONLY)

- Daily Practice
- Ask child to compose with the Movable Alphabet

CONSONANT DIGRAPHS + BEGINNING VOWEL DIGRAPHS

ch, sh, th, ee, oo as in book and oo as in moon

LESSON OF THE WEEK

sh

Explicit teaching: Sometimes two letters make one sound. S-H is two letters but one sound, /sh/

The letters s and h together say "sh" like in ship and shoe. It is two letters but just one sound. Let me show you how to spell SHIP.
Can you think of other words that start with SH?

DAILY PRACTICE

- Practice phonological awareness
- Read phonogram booklet
- Read sight word booklet
- Teach new sight words

SIGHT WORDS OF THE WEEK
down, what, from

SENTENCES OF THE WEEK:

The trash is by the shed.

That bag smells of fish.

DAY 1

- Daily practice
- Teach lesson of the week
- Dictate words:
  fish, shop, crash, shell, diminish, publish
- Word build:
  rash - dash - dish - fish - wish

DAY 2

- Daily practice
- Review lesson of the week
- Dictate sentences of the week

DAY 3

- Daily practice
- Ask child to read Sentences of the Week
- Ask child to read: Dot and Dan (Emergent Reader Book 9)
- Engage in a comprehension conversation:
  - What does Dot do while Dan naps?
  - How does Dan feel when he learns what Dot did?

DAY 4
(CHILDREN'S HOUSE ONLY)

- Daily Practice
- Ask child to compose with the Movable Alphabet

CONSONANT DIGRAPHS + BEGINNING VOWEL DIGRAPHS

ch, sh, th, ee, oo as in book and oo as in moon

LESSON OF THE WEEK

ee

Ee says e as in tree, bee, and free.
(others: fee, see, agree, glee)

When we put e and e together in ee, it says /ee/ like tree, bee, and free

---

DAILY PRACTICE

- Practice phonological awareness
- Read phonogram booklet
- Read sight word booklet
- Teach new sight words

SIGHT WORDS OF THE WEEK
birthday, do, their

SENTENCES OF THE WEEK:

The bee was so fast.

The keys fell in the street.

DAY 1

- Daily practice
- Teach lesson of the week
- Dictate words:
  bee, see, feet, tree, free, coffee *(okay if spelled with only one f)*
- Word build:
  bee - see - fee - tee - tree - free

DAY 2

- Daily practice
- Review lesson of the week
- Dictate sentences of the week

DAY 3

- Daily practice
- Ask child to read Sentences of the Week
- Ask child to read: Ted Can Do Tricks (Flyleaf Emergent Reader 15)
- Engage in a comprehension conversation:
  - What does Nel think about the dog?
  - Which trick did you like the most?

DAY 4 (CHILDREN'S HOUSE ONLY)

- Daily Practice
- Ask child to compose with the Movable Alphabet

CONSONANT DIGRAPHS + BEGINNING VOWEL DIGRAPHS

ch, sh, th, ee, oo as in book and oo as in moon

LEVEL
3
WEEK 4

LESSON OF THE WEEK

th

Teach: Remember ch and sh? We have another letter to put with h to make a new sound - a t! When we put t and h together they say "th". Can you think of any words that have th in them? Think is one!

DANGER (box)

DAILY PRACTICE

- Practice phonological awareness
- Read phonogram booklet
- Read sight word booklet
- Teach new sight words

SIGHT WORDS OF THE WEEK

they, away, are

SENTENCES OF THE WEEK:

What is on my bed?

Do you see the moth down the path?

Can you tell thick from thin?

DAY 1

- Daily practice
- Teach lesson of the week
- Dictate words:
  thud, math, path, thick, athletic, thicken
- Word build:
  thud - mud - mad - math - path

DAY 2

- Daily practice
- Review lesson of the week
- Dictate sentences of the week

DAY 3

- Daily practice
- Ask child to read Sentences of the Week
- Ask child to read: Dot Likes to Dig (Emergent Reader 10)
- Engage in a comprehension conversation:
  - How does Dan feel when he sees what Dot did?

DAY 4
(CHILDREN'S HOUSE ONLY)

- Daily Practice
- Ask child to compose with the Movable Alphabet

CONSONANT DIGRAPHS + BEGINNING VOWEL DIGRAPHS

ch, sh, th, ee, oo as in book and oo as in moon

LESSON OF THE WEEK

oo as in book

When we put o and o together in oo, one of the sounds it makes is
/oo/ in book and look.

DAY 1

- Daily practice
- Teach lesson of the week
- Dictate words:
  book, shook, wool, foot, football
- Word build:
  hook - book - look - took - shook

> # DAILY PRACTICE
>
> - Practice phonological awareness
> - Read phonogram booklet
> - Read sight word booklet
> - Teach new sight words
>
> ### SIGHT WORDS OF THE WEEK
> put, bear, puzzle

DAY 2

- Daily practice
- Review lesson of the week
- Dictate sentences of the week

DAY 3

- Daily practice
- Ask child to read Sentences of the Week
- Ask child to read: Hal Likes Hats (Flyleaf Emergent Reader 13)
- Engage in a comprehension conversation

SENTENCES OF THE WEEK:

Put the bear in my room.

I made a puzzle that looks like a broom.

DAY 4
(CHILDREN'S HOUSE ONLY)

- Daily Practice
- Ask child to compose with the Movable Alphabet

CONSONANT DIGRAPHS + BEGINNING VOWEL DIGRAPHS

ch, sh, th, ee, oo as in book and oo as in moon

LESSON OF THE WEEK

oo as in moon

Last week we talked about putting o and o together to make the sound in book and look. Did you know those two letters can also make another sound? They can sound like /ew/ as in spoon and moon.

DAILY PRACTICE

- Practice phonological awareness
- Read phonogram booklet
- Read sight word booklet
- Teach new sight words

SIGHT WORDS OF THE WEEK
great, giving, said

SENTENCES OF THE WEEK:

We meet in the classroom.

I cannot see the moon at noon.

DAY 1

- Daily practice
- Teach lesson of the week
- Dictate words:
  roof, room, zoom, moon, noon, classroom
- Word build:
  roof - room - zoom - loom - loon - noon

DAY 2

- Daily practice
- Review lesson of the week
- Dictate sentences of the week

DAY 3

- Daily practice
- Ask child to read Sentences of the Week
- Ask child to read: Fran Can Flip (Flyleaf Emergent Reader 14)
- Engage in a comprehension conversation:
  - We learn a lot about Fran's talents throughout the story. What are some of the things Fran can do?

DAY 4
(CHILDREN'S HOUSE ONLY)

- Daily Practice
- Ask child to compose with the Movable Alphabet

LEVEL 4

VOWEL DIGRAPHS

silent E, ay, ie, oa, oy

SIGHT WORDS

was, keys, so, sleepy, there, where, walking, window, new, goes, out, who, would, break, many, idea, solve, each

Level	Phonological Awareness (ORAL)	Writing (Encoding) & Reading (Decoding) Work	
		Phonics Elements to Focus on	**Sight Words / Puzzle Words**
4 6 weeks	1. Identify a Rhyme 2. Isolate Beginning Sound 3. Isolate Final Sound 4. Isolate Medial Sound 5. Blend Phonemes 6. Segment Phonemes 7. Generate a Rhyme 8. Compound Words: Delete First Word 9. Compound Words: Delete Second Word 10. Delete Beginning Sound 11. Delete Final Sound	**VOWEL DIGRAPHS:** silent E, ay, ie, oa, oy	was, keys, so, sleepy, there, where, walking, window, new, goes, out, who, would, break, many, idea, solve, each

VOWEL DIGRAPHS

silent E, ay, ie, oa, oy

LESSON OF THE WEEK

Silent e with u, i

Some people call silent E "magic e" because it changes the vowel sound! It makes the vowel say its name. Let's add an e to these words to see how the e changes the vowel.

cut - cute   cub - cube   tub - tube

It works the same for silent e with the vowel i. Let's add an e to these short i words to see how the e changes the vowel.

fin - fine   Tim - time   dim - dime
kit - kite   hid - hide

DAILY PRACTICE

- Practice phonological awareness
- Read phonogram booklet
- Read sight word booklet
- Teach new sight words

SIGHT WORDS OF THE WEEK
was, keys, so

SENTENCES OF THE WEEK:

The cats are cute.

We slide away in the tube.

DAY 1

- Daily practice
- Teach lesson of the week
- Dictate words:
  tune, cube, clue, cute, time, dime, slime, true
- Word build:
  tune - tine - fine - dine - dune

DAY 2

- Daily practice
- Review lesson of the week
- Dictate sentences of the week

DAY 3

- Daily practice
- Ask child to read Sentences of the Week
- Ask child to read: On a Log (Emergent Reader Book 12)
- Engage in a comprehension conversation:
  - What is on the very top of the pile before everyone falls?

DAY 4
(CHILDREN'S HOUSE ONLY)

- Daily Practice
- Ask child to compose with the Movable Alphabet

VOWEL DIGRAPHS

silent E, ay, ie, oa, oy

LESSON OF THE WEEK

silent e with o and a

Some people call silent E "magic e" because it changes the vowel sound! It makes the vowel say its name. Let's add an e to these words to see how the e changes the vowel.

hop - hope	mop - mope	cod - code
con - cone	rob - robe	rod - rode
not - note	tot - tote	slop - slope

It works the same for silent e with the vowel a. Let's add an e to these short a words to see how the e changes the vowel.

cap - cape	can - cane	rat - rate
mad - made	Sam - same	plan - plane
stat - state	scrap - scrape	

DAILY PRACTICE

- Practice phonological awareness
- Read phonogram booklet
- Read sight word booklet
- Teach new sight words

SIGHT WORDS OF THE WEEK
sleepy, there, where

SENTENCES OF THE WEEK:

Do you hope for a fun birthday gift?

What is on the cape?

DAY 1

- Daily practice
- Teach lesson of the week
- Dictate words:
  hope, mope, slope, plane, tape, cane, homemade
- Word build:
  hop - hope - mope - mop - lop - lope

DAY 2

- Daily practice
- Review lesson of the week
- Dictate sentences of the week

DAY 3

- Daily practice
- Ask child to read Sentences of the Week
- Ask child to read: To The Top (Emergent Reader 11)
- Engage in a comprehension conversation:
  - What do you think the Ram is thinking when he says "You can't top me, little ant. I am a ram!"?

DAY 4
(CHILDREN'S HOUSE ONLY)

- Daily Practice
- Ask child to compose with the Movable Alphabet

VOWEL DIGRAPHS

silent E, ay, ie, oa, oy

LESSON OF THE WEEK

ay

When we put the letters a and y together, they make the sound /ay/ as in way, play, say, and fray.

DAILY PRACTICE

- Practice phonological awareness
- Read phonogram booklet
- Read sight word booklet
- Teach new sight words

SIGHT WORDS OF THE WEEK
walking, window, new

SENTENCES OF THE WEEK:

Where can we play in hay?

If you are sleepy, go lay there.

DAY 1

- Daily practice
- Teach lesson of the week
- Dictate words:
  hay, day, lay, play, stay, holiday
- Word build:
  day - lay - pay - play - pray

DAY 2

- Daily practice
- Review lesson of the week
- Dictate sentences of the week

DAY 3

- Daily practice
- Ask child to read Sentences of the Week
- Ask child to read: The Sunset Pond (Emergent Reader 17)
- Engage in a comprehension conversation:
  - What does Bud see in the pond?
  - What does he do when he sees the frog?
  - Is he able to catch the frog?
  - How do you know?

DAY 4
(CHILDREN'S HOUSE ONLY)

- Daily Practice
- Ask child to compose with the Movable Alphabet

VOWEL DIGRAPHS

silent E, ay, ie, oa, oy

LEVEL 4 WEEK 4

LESSON OF THE WEEK

oa

When we put the letters o and a together, they make the sound /oa/ as in boat, float, and and goat.

DAILY PRACTICE

- Practice phonological awareness
- Read phonogram booklet
- Read sight word booklet
- Teach new sight words

SIGHT WORDS OF THE WEEK
goes, out, who

SENTENCES OF THE WEEK:

I am walking with my new coat on.

I can see the new road from my window.

DAY 1

- Daily practice
- Teach lesson of the week
- Dictate words:
  oat, coat, boat, goat, road, toad, toadstool
- Word build:
  oat - coat - goat - goad - toad

DAY 2

- Daily practice
- Review lesson of the week
- Dictate sentences of the week

DAY 3

- Daily practice
- Ask child to read Sentences of the Week
- Ask child to read: Jen's Best Gift Ever
  (Flyleaf Emergent Reader 18)
- Engage in a comprehension conversation:
  - What did Jen receive for her birthday?
  - What is the problem in the story?
  - How does Jen solve the problem?

DAY 4
(CHILDREN'S HOUSE ONLY)

- Daily Practice
- Ask child to compose with the Movable Alphabet

VOWEL DIGRAPHS

silent E, ay, ie, oa, oy

LESSON OF THE WEEK

ie

When we put the letters i and e together, they make the sound /ie/ as in pie, lie, and tie.

DAILY PRACTICE

- Practice phonological awareness
- Read phonogram booklet
- Read sight word booklet
- Teach new sight words

SIGHT WORDS OF THE WEEK
would, break, many

SENTENCES OF THE WEEK:

Who had pie for lunch?

He goes out to lie in the sun.

DAY 1

- Daily practice
- Teach lesson of the week
- Dictate words:
  tie, die, pie, pies, flies, sundried
- Word build:
  tie - pie - pies - lies - lied - flied

DAY 2

- Daily practice
- Review lesson of the week
- Dictate sentences of the week

DAY 3

- Daily practice
- Ask child to read Sentences of the Week
- Ask child to read: Will is Up at Bat (Emergent Reader 24)
- Engage in a comprehension conversation:
  - When Will gets a hit, where does the ball land?
  - Describe how Will gets to the base.

DAY 4
(CHILDREN'S HOUSE ONLY)

- Daily Practice
- Ask child to compose with the Movable Alphabet

VOWEL DIGRAPHS

silent E, ay, ie, oa, oy

LESSON OF THE WEEK

oy

When we put the letters o and y together, they make the sound /oy/ as in boy, toy, and joy.

DAILY PRACTICE

- Practice phonological awareness
- Read phonogram booklet
- Read sight word booklet
- Teach new sight words

SIGHT WORDS OF THE WEEK
idea, solve, each

SENTENCES OF THE WEEK:

This toy can break.

I would like to play with many toys.

DAY 1

- Daily practice
- Teach lesson of the week
- Dictate words:
  toy, joy, soy, busboy, batboy
- Word build:
  toy - boy - soy - joy

DAY 2

- Daily practice
- Review lesson of the week
- Dictate sentences of the week

DAY 3

- Daily practice
- Ask child to read Sentences of the Week
- Ask child to read: Meg and Jim's Sled trip (Flyleaf Emergent Reader 28)
- Engage in a comprehension conversation:
  - Why do you think Meg and Jim thought that it was a fantastic day to sled?
  - What causes Meg and Jim to fly out of the sled?
  - Why do Meg and Jim stop sledding?

DAY 4
(CHILDREN'S HOUSE ONLY)

- Daily Practice
- Ask child to compose with the Movable Alphabet

LEVEL 5

R CONTROLLED VOWELS AND INFLECTIONAL ENDINGS ED AND ING

R controlled vowels ar, or, ir, er, + inflectional endings ed and ing

Level	Phonological Awareness (ORAL)	Writing (Encoding) & Reading (Decoding) Work	
		Phonics Elements to Focus on	Sight Words / Puzzle Words
5 6 weeks	1. Identify a Rhyme 2. Isolate Beginning Sound 3. Isolate Final Sound 4. Isolate Medial Sound 5. Blend Phonemes 6. Segment Phonemes 7. Generate a Rhyme 8. Compound Words: Delete First Word 9. Compound Words: Delete Second Word 10. Delete Beginning Sound 11. Delete Final Sound	**R CONTROLLED VOWELS + INFLECTIONAL ENDINGS ED + ING:** ar, or, ir, er, + inflectional endings -ed and -ing	treasure, other, each, which, them, use, many, some, come, long, been, number, people, first, find, who, two, more

R CONTROLLED VOWELS AND INFLECTIONAL ENDINGS
ED and ING

*R controlled vowels ar, or, ir, er, + inflectional endings
ed and ing*

LESSON OF THE WEEK

r-controlled vowel spelled er

R-Controlled Vowels are often referred to as the
"**Strong R**" because the r causes the vowel to
change its sound. When the letter r follows a
vowel, the vowel and the /r/ make a new word,
changing the vowel sound.

When you see e and r together, think of them as a
team that says "er"

gem - germ   bet - Bert   her - herd

When we just have an r, we say /r/. When we put
the e and the r together, it says /er/.

DAILY PRACTICE

- Practice phonological awareness
- Read phonogram booklet
- Read sight word booklet
- Teach new sight words

SIGHT WORDS OF THE WEEK
teacher, have, love

SENTENCES OF THE WEEK:

The clerk can solve each idea.

The tiger is faster than I am.

DAY 1

- Daily practice
- Teach lesson of the week
- Dictate words:
  her, ferns, clerk, under, faster
- Word build:
  her - herd - nerd - nerds - herds

DAY 2

- Daily practice
- Review lesson of the week
- Dictate sentences of the week

DAY 3

- Daily practice
- Ask child to read Sentences of the Week
- Ask child to read: We Give Away
  (https://www.readinga-z.com/books/leveled-books/book/?id=1630&langId=1)
- Engage in a comprehension conversation:
  - What were some things they gave away?
  - Why do you think he couldn't give the bear away?
  - Have you ever given your things away?

DAY 4
(CHILDREN'S HOUSE ONLY)

- Daily Practice
- Ask child to compose with the Movable Alphabet

R CONTROLLED VOWELS AND INFLECTIONAL ENDINGS ED and ING

R controlled vowels ar, or, ir, er, + inflectional endings
ed and ing

LESSON OF THE WEEK

r-controlled vowels spelled ar

R-Controlled Vowels are often referred to as the "**Strong R**" because the r causes the vowel to change its sound. When the letter r follows a vowel, the vowel and the /r/ make a new word, changing the vowel sound.

ar says r

cat - cart   pat - part   mat - mart

When we just have an r, we say /r/. When we put the a and the r together, it says /ar/.

DAILY PRACTICE

- Practice phonological awareness
- Read phonogram booklet
- Read sight word booklet
- Teach new sight words

SIGHT WORDS OF THE WEEK
pull, our, want

SENTENCES OF THE WEEK:

I have to drive my car to the market.

I love my teachers and they love me!

DAY 1

- Daily practice
- Teach lesson of the week
- Dictate words:
  farm, harm, arms, market, target
- Word build:
  car - far - tar - star - stars

DAY 2

- Daily practice
- Review lesson of the week
- Dictate sentences of the week

DAY 3

- Daily practice
- Ask child to read Sentences of the Week
- Ask child to read: Ms. Rhonda's Readers: Pockets (*oo words: zoo, Kangaroo*)
- Engage in a comprehension conversation:
  - Why do you think the class fills up their pockets to go to the zoo?
  - What does the author mean when she writes that the kangaroo has the best pockets?

DAY 4 (CHILDREN'S HOUSE ONLY)

- Daily Practice
- Ask child to compose with the Movable Alphabet

R CONTROLLED VOWELS AND INFLECTIONAL ENDINGS
ED and ING

R controlled vowels ar, or, ir, er, + inflectional endings ed and ing

LESSON OF THE WEEK

r-controlled vowels spelled or

Explicit Teaching:
R-Controlled Vowels are often referred to as the "**Strong R**" because the r causes the vowel to change its sound. When the letter r follows a vowel, the vowel and the /r/ make a new word, changing the vowel sound.

or says or as in for

spots - sports   pot - port   for - fort

When we just have an r, we say /r/. When we put the o and the r together, it says /or/.

DAILY PRACTICE

- Practice phonological awareness
- Read phonogram booklet
- Read sight word booklet
- Teach new sight words

SIGHT WORDS OF THE WEEK
were, blue, lucky

SENTENCES OF THE WEEK:

I want to pull the corn off the cob.

We want to decorate our new bikes with horns.

DAY 1

- Daily practice
- Teach lesson of the week
- Dictate words:
  born, corn, fort, fork, short, decorate
- Word build:
  for - fort - fork - stork - storks

DAY 2

- Daily practice
- Review lesson of the week
- Dictate sentences of the week

DAY 3

- Daily practice
- Ask child to read Sentences of the Week
- Ask child to read: Little Loon (https://www.readinga-z.com/books/leveled-books/book/?id=1630&langId=1)
- Engage in a comprehension conversation

DAY 4
(CHILDREN'S HOUSE ONLY)

- Daily Practice
- Ask child to compose with the Movable Alphabet

R CONTROLLED VOWELS AND INFLECTIONAL ENDINGS
ED and ING

R controlled vowels ar, or, ir, er, + inflectional endings
ed and ing

LESSON OF THE WEEK

r controlled vowels spelled ir

Explicit Teaching:
R-Controlled Vowels are often referred to as the **"Strong R"** because the r causes the vowel to change its sound. When the letter r follows a vowel, the vowel and the /r/ make a new word, changing the vowel sound.

ir says ir as in dirt

first - first   skit - skirt   chip - chirp

When we just have an r, we say /r/. When we put the i and the r together, it says /er/. That's just like the e and the r together! We will have to pay close attention during our reading to see when /er/ is spelled with an er versus an ir. This week, we will be working with ir.

DAILY PRACTICE

- Practice phonological awareness
- Read phonogram booklet
- Read sight word booklet
- Teach new sight words

SIGHT WORDS OF THE WEEK
over, your, four

SENTENCES OF THE WEEK:

The blue birds were on a tree.
The girl got dirt on her lucky skirt.

DAY 1

- Daily practice
- Teach lesson of the week
- Dictate words:
  stir, dirt, skirt, girl, first, thirteenth
- Word build:
  fir - firm - form - bird - birch - birth

DAY 2

- Daily practice
- Review lesson of the week
- Dictate sentences of the week

DAY 3

- Daily practice
- Ask child to read Sentences of the Week
- Ask child to read: Ms. Rhonda's Readers: Kittens
- Engage in a comprehension conversation:
  - Who owns the mama cat?
  - How many kittens does the cat have?
  - What are some things the kittens do when they are playing?
  - Who takes one of the kittens at the end of the story? (Mika)

DAY 4
(CHILDREN'S HOUSE ONLY)

- Daily Practice
- Ask child to compose with the Movable Alphabet

R CONTROLLED VOWELS AND INFLECTIONAL ENDINGS
ED and ING

R controlled vowels ar, or, ir, er, + inflectional endings ed and ing

LESSON OF THE WEEK

past tense ed

past tense -ed makes three sounds (t as in jumped, d as in played, and ed as in planted)

First spell the base word and then add -ed. Sometimes you will double the consonant, but not in the examples we are working with this week.

DAILY PRACTICE

- Practice phonological awareness
- Read phonogram booklet
- Read sight word booklet
- Teach new sight words

SIGHT WORDS OF THE WEEK
these, could, why

SENTENCES OF THE WEEK:

I walked over to your garden.

I played with my four sisters.

DAY 1

- Daily practice
- Teach lesson of the week
- Build these phonetically regular words and then add -ed

walk - walked	kiss - kissed
look - looked	play - played
start - started	jump - jumped
plant - planted	

DAY 2

- Daily practice
- Review lesson of the week
- Dictate sentences of the week

DAY 3

- Daily practice
- Ask child to read Sentences of the Week
- Ask child to read: Bath Time (https://www.readinga-z.com/books/leveled-books/book/?id=662&langId=1)
- Engage in a comprehension conversation

DAY 4
(CHILDREN'S HOUSE ONLY)

- Daily Practice
- Ask child to compose with the Movable Alphabet

R CONTROLLED VOWELS AND INFLECTIONAL ENDINGS
ED and ING

R controlled vowels ar, or, ir, er, + inflectional endings ed and ing

LEVEL 5 WEEK 6

LESSON OF THE WEEK

ing as an inflectional ending and a

This week we are going to put three letters together! When we put an i, n, and g together, we can sound it out slowly as /i-n-g/. But when we read it more smoothly, it sounds like /ing/.

DAILY PRACTICE

- Practice phonological awareness
- Read phonogram booklet
- Read sight word booklet
- Teach new sight words

SIGHT WORDS OF THE WEEK
one, very, please

SENTENCES OF THE WEEK:

Why are these children not singing?

Could you bring me the rings?

DAY 1

- Daily practice
- Teach lesson of the week
- Dictate words
  sing, ring, spring, bring, springing

walk - walking	kiss - kissing
look - looking	play - playing
start - starting	jump- jumping
plant - planting	

DAY 2

- Daily practice
- Review lesson of the week
- Dictate sentences of the week

DAY 3

- Daily practice
- Ask child to read Sentences of the Week
- Ask child to read: The Class Pet (https://www.readinga-z.com/books/leveled-books/book/?id=3078&langId=1)
- Engage in a comprehension conversation

DAY 4
(CHILDREN'S HOUSE ONLY)

- Daily Practice
- Ask child to compose with the Movable Alphabet

PHONOLOGICAL AWARENESS APPENDIX

Phonological Awareness Appendix

Identify a Rhyme - Thumbs up/down, eyes open/closed, yes/no, etc.

tap, cap bat, sad bag, rag can, cap cat, sat	fix, mix big, pig did, dig fit, sit hid, lid	mop, pop cap, cat dip, sip dot, Don dig, pig	will, pill fin, tin fat, rat fig, pit hop, mop	net, met hen, pen fan, ran the, see we, did	tin, win fan, nap no, try ten, men hop, mop	zip, lip tall, wall duck, cat wet, jet bug, mop	bad, rag mad, dad lip, lit pill, hill rip, sip	my, you sad, dad see, too play, may low, slow
cob, job Don, Ron gob, got hot, not Knob, jot	box, fox big, fig can, man dad, rat fan, nap	tax, wax tap, map big, wig yes, me tag, bag	hi, go hut, him lot, pot ran, fan big, pig	sick, pick mat, cat gum, can wet, jet mad, dad	hot, cup bad, not red, bed fit, tub sox, box	tin, tip win, pin box, fox sob, got bop, Bob	zip, lip hot, pot fun, run map, dad big, pig	sat, mat set, ham bed, fed mop, hop bit, fit
grip, trip grin, green bread, head gruff, grow prop, drop	span, scan stinky, slinky snack, still slug, slap swell, smell	drum, from branch, bring frog, front trap, try dunk, trunk	slap, snap snack, stink swift, snip stick, slick slip, sled	last, chat with, win rich, pitch this, chill thin, chin	whip, chip slim, slow flop, plop glad, pad slop, clop	plus, glob clop, slop flip, flat blue, glue fly, flag	slip, slob sled, bled flag, slug flap, clap glob, slob	flee, glee fly, sly clay, play clad, grin clue, blue
flip, clip plan, plain glad, plaid slow, slim flap, slap	bless, slush flash, plug flop, plop click, slick class, glass	slop, clop flash, flush slip, clip blend, bland plant, slant	blush, slush flap, clump clock, clap black, slack gloss, floss	slim, plate clam, slam clump, slump slip, slob flag, slug	plant, plot sled, bled flash, clash slush, flip glob, slob	black, flack plug, slug slim, flag slick, flick flash, glitch	flap, clap clam, slop glob, slob clump, clamp blush, flush	clip, slip plus, glob plump, glump flip, flat clop, slop
chip, miss this, trip that, flat chip, ship wish, dish	skate, date loud, proud churn, look beach, reach shook, turn	cross, crow crack, track bring, broke brisk, frisk trip, train	seal, real smoke, flip ship, truck clock, dock truck, stuck	splat, flat tail, night flash, smash snail, fright time, dime	guess, dress snack, black twist, draw shook, look fist, straw	brush, crush drip, trip grip, grape crop, drop trip, trap	spark, pink house, louse float, goat small, wall shark, drink	blow, flow slice, flap sleet, pleat clean, clay glade, blade

Fall /f/ Kids /k/ Gym /j/ Leg /l/ Mom /m/	Name /n/ Pick /p/ Queen kw Run /r/ See /s/	Boat /b/ Cat /k/ Desk /d/ Fall /f/ Good /g/	Talk /t/ Very /v/ Win /w/ Yell /y/ Zip /z/	Name /n/ Pig /p/ Quit /kw/ Rain /r/ See /s/	Toy /t/ Vase /v/ Week /w/ Yell /y/ Zip /z/	Home /h/ Jug /j/ Kind /k/ Look /l/ Mine /m/	Help /h/ Jump /j/ Kick /k/ Laugh /l/ Me /m/	Ball /b/ Cup /k/ Dig /d/ Fun /f/ Gas /g/
Big /b/ Can /k/ Did /d/ Fix /f/ Get /g/	Night /n/ Paint /p/ Quick /kw/ Room /r/ Soap /s/	Tub /t/ Vote /v/ Won /w/ Yellow /y/ Zoom /z/	Seat /s/ Nice /n/ Pup /p/ Run /r/ Top /t/	Big /b/ Can /k/ Did /d/ Fix /f/ Get /g/	Hair /h/ Juice /j/ Kiss /k/ Light /l/ Milk /m/	Quick /qw/ Zoo /z/ Van /v/ Wish /w/ Yes /y/	Talk /t/ Voice /v/ Water /w/ Zero /z/ You /y/	Hop /h/ Jam /j/ Keep /k/ Lip /l/ Make /m/
Ant /a/ At /a/ Me /m/ Apple /a/ Ask /a/	Antler /a/ Andy /a/ You /y/ After /a/ Dog /d/	It /i/ Big /b/ Itch /i/ Come /k/ If /i/	Nice /n/ Inside /i/ Pig /p/ It /i/ Itchy /i/	Ask /a/ Elbow /e/ Object /o/ Itch /i/ Exit /e/	Onto /o/ Save /s/ Ostrich /o/ After /a/ Odd /o/	In /i/ Object /o/ Inside /i/ Actor /a/ Ox /o/	Up /u/ And /a/ If /i/ On /o/ Under /u/	End /e/ Odd /o/ If /i/ On /o/ Elf /e/
Chest /ch/ Shed /sh/ This /th/ Shell /sh/ Thin /th/	When /wh/ Thunder /th/ Chin /ch/ That /th/ Whip /wh/	Shag /sh/ Which /wh/ Children /ch/ Thinner /th/ Whiz /wh/	Black /bl/ Clam /cl/ Glow /gl/ Plus /pl/ Slick /sl/	Clock /cl/ Sled /sl/ Flat /fl/ Blimp /bl/ Flip /fl/	Glad /gl/ Class /cl/ Block /bl/ Flick /fl/ Plant /pl/	Slump /sl/ Planet /pl/ Flag /fl/ Glue /gl/ Slush /sl/	Frill /fr/ Prop /pr/ Brush /br/ Crop /cr/ Drip /dr/	Frog /fr/ Grab /gr/ Press /pr/ Trap /tr/ Bread /br/
Bread /br/ Trap /tr/ Pray /pr/ Grades /gr/ Freeze /fr/	Drum /dr/ Brag /br/ Trip /tr/ Crab /cr/ Grant /gr/	Spice /sp/ Store /st/ Sweeter /sw/ Snore /sn/ Smoky /sm/	Smile /sm/ Swell /sw/ Spill /sp/ Stop /st/ Snub /sn/	Still /st/ Scab /sc/ Spot /sp/ Stuck /st/ Slot /sl/	Swing /sw/ Snack /sn/ Stomp /st/ Slept /sl/ Smug /sm/	Scrap /scr/ Split /spl/ Sprain /spr/ Square /skw/ Strap /str/	Sprint /spr/ Scrape /scr/ Straw /str/ Splice /spl/ Scream /scr/	Squash /skw/ Splat /spl/ Spread /spr/ Stream /str/ Splash /spl/

Isolate Final Sound - Repeat word then isolate or "punch out" the last sound

Job /b/ Bed /d/ Life /f/ Bug /g/ Page /j/	Book /k/ Ball /l/ Gum /m/ Can /n/ Tip /p/	Safe /f/ Egg /g/ Park /k/ Cage /j/ Doll /l/	Room /m/ Clap /p/ Eat /t/ Man /n/ Dress /s/	Mail /l/ Home /m/ Fun /n/ Skip /p/ Mad /d/	Hot /t/ Cave /v/ Freeze /z/ Rub /b/ Miss /s/	Soap /p/ Grass /s/ Foot /t/ Stove /v/ Froze /z/	Arm /m/ Loud /d/ Leaf /f/ Big /g/ Cab /b/	Cube /b/ Loud /d/ Knife /f/ Tag /g/ Large /j/
Yes /s/ Bat /t/ Give /v/ Buzz /z/ Tub /b/	Good /d/ Leaf /f/ Flag /g/ Like /k/ Huge /j/	Live /v/ Size /z/ Crib /b/ Stage /j/ Head /d/	Dime /m/ Top /p/ Dog /g/ Cough /f/ Ran /n/	Knife /f/ Bag /g/ Fudge /j/ Clock /k/ Hall /l/	Time /m/ Move /v/ Ship /p/ Great /t/ Pen /n/	Sob /b/ Hid /d/ Cuff /f/ Rag /g/ Fix /ks/	Pick /k/ Bell /l/ Came /m/ Tan /n/ Sip /p/	Dress /s/ Coat /t/ Sleeve /v/ Fox /x/ Was /z/
Smile /l/ Game /m/ Run /n/ Stop /p/ Class /s/	Coat /t/ Red /d/ Fuzz /z/ Job /b/ Have /v/	Kiss /s/ Hat /t/ Drive /v/ Prize /z/ Web /b/	Lid /d/ Roof /f/ Leg /g/ Large /j/ Cook /k/	Scrub /b/ Mile /l/ Half /f/ Rain /n/ Rise /z/	Charge /j/ Lake /k/ Ride /d/ Team /m/ Dig /g/	Bus /s/ Let /t/ Five /v/ Box /ks/ Buzz /z/	Robe /b/ Made /d/ Life /f/ Tug /g/ Cake /k/	Box /ks/ Mall /l/ Stem /m/ Green /n/ Ship /p/
Then /n/ Roof /f/ Log /g/ Sail /l/ Bird /d/	Close /s/ Block /k/ Slope /p/ Flag /g/ Plus /s/	Jump /p/ Leaf /f/ Vase /s/ Desk /k/ Five /v/	Plum /m/ Sheep /p/ Blaze /z/ Steak /k/ Cliff /f/	Sleek /k/ Whole /l/ Have /v/ Flood /d/ Blink /k/	Flame /m/ Gift /t/ Flex /x/ Cup /p/ Work /k/	Shrub /b/ Float /t/ Then /n/ Wolf /f/ Zoom /m/	Nine /n/ Flag /g/ Sub /b/ Sled /d/ Ball /l/	Sleeve /v/ Shout /t/ Some /m/ Flown /n/ Off /f/
Cook /k/ Him /m/ Have /v/ Fig /g/ So /o/	Web /b/ Ball /l/ Test /t/ Laugh /f/ Fun /n/	Fuzz /z/ Neck /k/ Mess /s/ Lead /d/ Ham /m/	Six /x/ Age /j/ Cap /p/ Take /k/ Hill /l/	Class /s/ Pack /k/ Crumb /m/ Give /v/ Cuff /f/	Mop /p/ Tub /b/ Wall /l/ Hat /t/ Ride /d/	Love /v/ Twig /g/ Know /o/ Crib /b/ Cage /j/	Hen /n/ Ox /x/ Huge /j/ Rope /p/ Cab /b/	Throw /o/ Buzz /z/ Pick /k/ Less /s/ Duck /k/
Smooth /th/ Pinch /ch/ North /th/ Crash /sh/	Reach /ch/ Patch /ch/ Wreath /th/ Dish /sh/	Teach /ch/ Whoosh /sh/ Health /th/ Finish /sh/	Fresh /sh/ South /th/ Wash /sh/ Rich /ch/	Bush /sh/ Church /ch/ Both /th/ Leash /sh/	Plush /sh/ With /th/ Gush /sh/ Booth /th/	Mash /sh/ Breath /th/ Witch /ch/ Path /th/	Ditch /ch/ Ninth /th/ Flash /sh/ Tooth /th/	Mouth /th/ Polish /sh/ Fifth /th/ Touch /ch/

cAt	jIg	mOm	bUm	sAt	dId	jOb	hAt	mUd
mAp	sIt	fIt	jUt	hIll	rOd	mOm	kId	hUff
bAg	kIss	gAs	toUgh	dOt	bIg	lOt	lOt	fUn
cAn	rId	lOck	dUck	vAn	mAd	mOp	mAp	cUb
bAck	tIck	bIt	sUb	fIx	mIss	nOt	fIll	bUd
dOt	pOt	kId	pUff	gAg	hIt	fOx	rAm	cUt
cOp	wAx	rIg	hUt	fAn	rIp	zAp	hAt	gUsh
rOd	hId	hIll	gUm	lAck	fIx	fIt	cAp	yUck
gOt	knOb	sIck	cUt	bAd	hIss	rOck	nAg	sUn
jOb	sAd	hIp	bUt	jAb	JIm	tAp	mAn	rUb
pAck	pIg	hIt	nAp	BOb	bOx	pIll	dOt	jUg
hAd	sIp	pOp	tAg	cOb	pAn	lIp	fOx	gUn
tAb	hIs	hAm	pAn	lOt	dIg	pIn	gOt	dUg
bAm	lIck	rIp	sAck	mOp	gOb	fIb	hOp	bUzz
mAt	TIm	dOll	mAd	lObk	wAg	hId	hOt	bUg
nUt	dUg	dOll	dAd	mUd	bAt	fUzz	fAn	bUzz
hUsh	rAn	hOp	cAb	rUsh	fIn	hUt	hId	cAt
lUck	nUt	pOt	hAm	nUmb	sOck	fIll	dOll	dIp
sUm	bIg	ROb	fAt	tUg	bUd	rOck	tUg	sOb
pUp	tOp	TOm	lAp	rUn	tUg	fUss	cUb	pUp
bUg	bUn	fAn	bEt	wEt	lEd	gUm	cUp	fUn
tAp	fOx	cUt	mOp	dIg	rAn	dAd	sAd	mAn
pIg	fIt	hOp	fIb	jOb	nOt	hIm	mIx	fIn
mOp	tUb	lEt	hEn	rIp	tUb	lOt	pOt	cOt
sUb	lIp	dIp	tAg	fUn	pAn	sUn	mUd	hUg

B-e be B-i by S-a say S-o so H-a hay	G-o go H-e he W-e we H-i hi M-a may	S-e see M-i my T-o toe L-a lay M-e me	p-i pie l-o low d-a day f-e fee s-i sigh	P-a pay N-e knee L-i lie D-o doe W-a way	J-o Joe r-a ray n-o no t-i tie w-i why	y-oo you h-e he t-o toe J-a Jay z-oo zoo	L-i-p lip T-u-b tub F-i-t fit F-o-x fox B-u-n bun
D-a-b dab H-a-m ham W-a-g wag R-a-t rat L-a-p lap	B-e-g beg F-e-d fed L-e-d led P-e-n pen G-e-t get	M-u-d mud P-o-t pot M-i-x mix S-a-d sad K-u-p cup	H-a-z has W-a-x wax S-a-d sad M-a-t mat C-a-b cab	D-i-g dig L-i-k lick D-i-m dim S-i-p sip F-i-n fin	P-a-t pat S-a-p sap V-a-n van Z-a-p zap T-a-x tax	S-u-n sun L-o-k lock H-i-m him D-a-d dad G-u-m gum	T-o-p top B-i-g big N-u-t nut R-a-n ran D-u-g dug
K-i-s kiss R-i-d rid W-i-n win Z-i-p zip F-i-l fill	P-u-p pup S-u-m sum L-u-k luck H-u-f huff N-u-t nut	S-u-b sub M-o-p mop P-i-g pig T-a-p tap B-u-g bug	B-u-n bun K-u-f cuff T-u-b tub R-u-g rug H-u-m hum	K-u-b cub T-u-g tug D-o-l doll H-i-d hid F-a-n fan	R-u-n run K-u-p cup G-u-t gut M-u-d mud S-u-b sub	D-i-d did Z-i-p zip B-i-g big H-i-t hit T-i-p tip	H-u-g hug K-o-t cot F-i-n fin M-a-n man F-u-n fun
ch-i-k chick th-a-n than sh-u-t shut sh-a-k shack ch-i-p chip	sh-e-l-f shelf ch-i-n chin th-i-s this wh-i-z whiz ch-i-ll chill	th-e-n then sh-e-l shell ch-u-m chum th-i-n thin ch-e-k cheek	sh-o-p shop wh-i-f whif ch-a-t chat th-i-s this wh-e-n when	wh-i-t white ch-o-p chop ch-e-z cheese ch-e-s-t chest th-i-n-k think	t-e-ch teach ch-o-k choke th-r-o throw sh-a-p shape wh-e-t wheat	s-t-e-m stem s-l-e-d sled s-t-i-k stick s-m-o-k smock s-n-a-p snap	s-k-u-l skull s-w-ing swing s-n-a-k snack s-l-e-p-t slept s-t-a-k stack
s-p-a-s space s-l-o-p slope s-w-e-t sweet s-n-a-k snake s-p-i-n spine	s-m-i-l smile s-l-i-d slide s-p-e-k speak s-t-a-k steak s-n-a-l snail	s-l-e-k sleek s-t-e-p steep s-p-i-d spied s-k-a-l scale s-w-a sway	b-r-u-sh brush c-r-e-m cream d-r-e-s dress f-r-i fry g-r-a-v-e gravy	p-r-e-s press t-r-a-d trade b-r-e-d bread c-r-o-p crop d-r-i-v drive	f-r-i-z fries g-r-a-s grass p-r-o-b probe t-r-a-l trail b-r-i-j bridge	g-r-i-p grip p-r-i-z prize t-r-a-v-l travel b-r-a-k brake c-r-a-sh crash	b-r-a-n brain f-r-o-g frog g-r-a-n-d grand p-r-i-t-e pretty t-r-a tray

s-p-l-a-sh splash c-r-i-s-p crisp p-r-e-s-e-n-t present b-l-a-n-k-e-t blanket	t-r-u-m-p-e-t trumpet g-r-ou-n-d ground s-l-e-p-e sleepy p-r-o-g-r-a-m program	ch-u-n-k-e chunky th-i-k-n-e-s thickness wh-i-s-p-er whisper r-i-s-t-w-o-ch wristwatch	ch-i-m-n-e chimney s-l-i-th-er slither s-u-n-sh-i-n sunshine ch-i-l-d-r-e-n children

Gum g-u-m Dad d-a-d Him h-i-m Lot l-o-t Sun s-u-n	Cup c-u-p Sad s-a-d Mix m-i-x Pot p-o-t Mud m-u-d	Bud b-u-d Cub c-u-b Fun f-u-n Huff h-u-f Mud m-u-d	Buzz b-u-z Hut h-u-t Fill f-i-l Rock r-o-k Fuss f-u-s	Led l-e-d Ran r-a-n Not n-o-t Tub t-u-b Leg l-e-g	Wet w-e-t Dig d-i-g Job j-o-b Fun f-u-n Met m-e-t	Pup p-u-p Sum s-u-m Luck l-u-k Sun s-u-n Nut n-u-t	Bun b-u-n Fox f-o-x Fit f-i-t Tub t-u-b Lip l-i-p
Bug b-u-g Tap t-a-p Pig p-i-g Mop m-o-p Sub s-u-b	Bell b-e-l Get g-e-t Leg l-e-g Met m-e-t Red r-e-d	Fun f-u-n Man m-a-n Fin f-i-n Cot c-o-t Hug h-u-g	Fix f-i-x Van v-a-n Dot d-o-t Hill h-i-l Sat s-a-t	Get g-e-t Fed f-e-d Ted t-e-d Beg b-e-g Vet v-e-t	Doll d-o-l Rip r-i-p Ham h-a-m Pop p-o-p Hit h-i-t	Fill f-i-l Rock r-o-k Fit f-i-t Zap z-a-p Fox f-o-x	Bat b-a-t Fin f-i-n Job j-o-b Bud b-u-d Tug t-u-g
Fan f-a-n Hid h-i-d Doll d-o-l Tug t-u-g Cub c-u-b	Fuzz f-u-z Cat c-a-t Dip d-i-p Sob s-o-b Pup p-u-p	Bet b-e-t Mop m-o-p Fib f-i-b Hen h-e-n Tag t-a-g	Fan f-a-n Cut c-u-t Yes y-e-s Let l-e-t Dip d-i-p	Wag w-a-g Gob g-o-b Dig d-i-g Pan p-a-n Box b-o-x	Miss m-i-s Mad m-a-d Big b-i-g Rod r-o-d Dig d-i-g	Dug d-u-g Ran r-a-n Nut n-u-t Big b-i-g Top t-o-p	His h-i-s Pad p-a-d Job j-o-b Lip l-i-p Ham h-a-m
chimp ch-i-m-p than th-a-n shut sh-u-t chip ch-i-p shelf sh-e-l-f	ship sh-i-p shack sh-a-k thick th-i-k thin th-i-n why wh-i	that th-a-t shed sh-e-d them th-e-m check ch-e-k which wh-i-ch	shell sh-e-l thump th-u-m-p when wh-e-n then th-e-n chin ch-i-n	wham wh-a-m chill ch-i-l them th-e-m wheat wh-e-t chest ch-e-s-t	thick th-i-k chef sh-e-f shock sh-o-k whop wh-o-p shut sh-u-t	thumb th-u-m this th-i-s white wh-i-t chop ch-o-p thank th-a-n-k	lunch l-u-n-ch finish f-i-n-i-sh brush b-r-u-sh breath b-r-e-th sheep sh-e-p
teeth t-e-th flash f-l-a-sh crash c-r-a-sh fifth f-i-f-th while wh-i-l	wheels wh-e-l-z shine sh-i-n thread th-r-e-d which wh-i-ch cheek ch-e-k	trade t-r-a-d bread b-r-e-d crop c-r-o-p drive d-r-i-v grass g-r-a-s	frog f-r-o-g tray t-r-a crab c-r-a-b freeze f-r-e-z print p-r-i-n-t	trap t-r-a-p braid b-r-a-d crack c-r-a-k drill d-r-i-l prize p-r-i-z	swam s-w-a-m step s-t-e-p skip s-k-i-p snob s-n-o-b snag s-n-a-g	slope s-l-o-p scale s-k-a-l sleet s-l-e-t snow s-n-o swipe s-w-i-p	split s-p-l-i-t straw s-t-r-aw screw s-c-r-oo splice s-p-l-i-s squeal s-kw-e-l

slipper s-l-i-p-er program p-r-o-g-r-a-m splinter s-p-l-i-n-t-er gravity g-r-a-v-i-t-e	climbed c-l-i-m-d twinkle t-w-i-n-k-l princess p-r-i-n-s-e-s blanket b-l-a-n-k-e-t	weather w-e-th-er whisper wh-i-s-p-er shaker sh-a-k-er ticklish t-i-k-l-i-sh	leather l-e-th-er shoulder sh-o-l-d-er wishbone w-i-sh-b-o-n checkers ch-e-k-er-s

Generate a Rhyme

-at: cat, bat, hat -ub: cub, hub, rub	-ap: map, nap, sap -uck: duck, luck	-ab: cab, fab, nab -ust: dust, must, trust	-am: ham, Sam, cam -ump: bump, dump, lump	-in: bin, fin, chin -ed: red, bed, shed	-it: bit, sit, fit -eg: leg, beg, Meg	-ist: mist, fist, wrist -est: best, west	-ish: dish, fish, wish -et: bet, vet, wet	-op: hop, cop, top -ub: cub, hub, rub
-ag: bag, gag, rag -ug: bug, rug, tug	-an: Dan, fan, tan -um: bum, gum, sum	-and: band sand -unk: junk, bunk	-ast: fast, last, cast -ush: rush, hush, mush	-ig: big, pig, fig -ell: tell, bell, shell	-ill: Bill, Jill, chill -eck: deck neck	-ot: pot, hot, not -ill: chill, bill, mill	-ob: Bob, job, cob -op: shop, mop, cop	-uck: duck, luck, truck -ug: bug, rug, tug
-ack: back, tack -un: sun, bun, fun	-ad: bad, Dad, had -ut: but, nut, cut	-ip: dip, rip, chip -en: hen, Ben, then	-id: bid, did, hid -et: met, set, net	-ick: wick, chick, sick -ess: mess less	-im: dim, him, rim -end: bend tend	-ock: dock, rock -ick: sick, chick, lick	-og: fog, dog, hog -ine: dine, mine, pine	-um: bum, gum, sum -un: sun, bun, fun
-ut: but, nut, cut -ust: dust, must, trust	-ump: bump, thump, stump -unk: junk, bunk, chunk	-ush: rush, hush, gush -en: hen, Ben, then	-et: met, set, net -ed: red, bed, shed	-eg: leg, beg, Meg -ell: tell, bell, shell	-eck: deck, neck, check -ess: mess, chess, less	-end: bend, mend, trend -est: best, west, chest	-et: bet, vet, wet -ake: bake, cake, flake	-ay: play, day, ray -eat/eet: feet, treat, street
-ing: bring, thing -ine: shine, nine, mine	-ice: twice, dice, rice -oor/ore: door, store	-ame: game, flame, name -ash: flash, splash, crash	-y: cry, shy, by, my -ale/ail: sale, mail	-ide/ied: side, tried, bide -oke/oak: soak, choke	-ank: tank, thank, rank -ow: show, snow, blow	-ink: wink, blink, think -e/ee: me, see, we	-ane/ain: train, plane -ight/ite: flight, bright	-ate/ait: plate, wait, fate -ock: sock, rock, clock

Compound Words: Delete First Word

Say baseball. Now say baseball but don't say base. >> ball	Say battleship. Now say battleship but don't say battle. >> ship	Say bedroom. Now say bedroom but don't say bed. >> room	Say bedspread. Now say bedspread but don't say bed. >> spread	Say bluebird. Now say bluebird but don't say blue. >> bird	Say breakfast. Now say breakfast but don't say break. >> fast	Say butterfly. Now say butterfly but don't say butter. >> fly	Say cardboard. Now say cardboard but don't say card. >> board
Say classroom. Now say classroom but don't say class. >> room	Say daytime. Now say daytime but don't say day. >> time	Say driveway. Now say driveway but don't say drive. >> way	Say everyone. Now say everyone but don't say every. >> one	Say everything. Now say everything but don't say every. >> thing	Say fishhook. Now say fishhook but don't say fish. >> hook	Say footstep. Now say footstep but don't say foot. >> step	Say pineapple. Now say pineapple but don't say pine. >> apple
Say gentleman. Now say gentleman but don't say gentle. >> man	Say grandfather. Now say grandfather but don't say grand. >> father	Say grandmother. Now say grandmother but don't say grand. >> mother	Say grapefruit. Now say grapefruit but don't say grape. >> fruit	Say graveyard. Now say graveyard but don't say grave. >> yard	Say handball. Now say handball but don't say hand. >> ball	Say haystack. Now say haystack but don't say hay. >> stack	Say headache. Now say headache but don't say head. >> ache
Say himself. Now say himself but don't say him. >> self	Say outside. Now say outside but don't say out >> side	Say outfit. Now say outfit but don't say out. >> fit	Say itself. Now say itself but don't say it. >> self	Say lookout. Now say lookout but don't say look. >> out	Say forget. Now say forget but don't say for. >> get	Say myself. Now say myself but don't say my. >> self	Say necktie. Now say necktie but don't say neck. >> tie
Say notebook. Now say notebook but don't say note. >> book	Say oatmeal. Now say oatmeal but don't say oat. >> meal	Say horseback. Now say horseback but don't say horse. >> back	Say homesick. Now say homesick but don't say home. >> sick	Say pancake. Now say pancake but don't say pan. >> cake	Say peanut. Now say peanut but don't say pea. >> nut	Say moonlight. Now say moonlight but don't say moon. >> light	Say playground. Now say playground but don't say play. >> ground
Say pocketbook. Now say pocketbook but don't say pocket >> book	Say popcorn. Now say popcorn but don't say pop. >> corn	Say railroad. Now say railroad but don't say rail. >> road	Say raincoat. Now say raincoat but don't say rain. >> coat	Say sailboat. Now say sailboat but don't say sail. >> boat	Say sidewalk. Now say sidewalk but don't say side. >> walk	Say snowball. Now say snowball but don't say snow. >> ball	Say snowflake. Now say snowflake but don't say snow. >> flake

Compound Words: Delete First Word

Say somebody. Now say somebody but don't say some. >> body	Say someone. Now say someone but don't say some. >> one	Say something. Now say something but don't say some. >> thing	Say sometimes. Now say sometimes but don't say some. >> times	Say somewhere. Now say somewhere but don't say some. >> where	Say strawberry. Now say strawberry but don't say straw. >> berry	Say streetcar. Now say streetcar but don't say street. >> car	Say sunshine. Now say sunshine but don't say sun. >> shine
Say anywhere. Now say anywhere but don't say any. >> where	Say understand. Now say understand but don't say under. >> stand	Say understood. Now say understood but don't say under. >> stood	Say washtub. Now say washtub but don't say wash. >> tub	Say wastebasket. Now say wastebasket but don't say waste. >> basket	Say greyhound. Now say greyhound but don't say grey. >> hound	Say workshop. Now say workshop but don't say work. >> shop	Say yourself. Now say yourself but don't say your. >> self
Say mailbox. Now say mailbox but don't say mail. >> box	Say goldfish. Now say goldfish but don't say gold. >> fish	Say anything. Now say anything but don't say any. >> thing	Say coconut. Now say coconut but don't say coco. >> nut	Say backpack. Now say backpack but don't say back. >> pack	Say become. Now say become but don't say be. >> come	Say everywhere. Now say everywhere but don't say every. >> where	Say deckhand. Now say deckhand but don't say deck >> hand
Say outlaw. Now say outlaw but don't say out. >> law	Say tonight. Now say tonight but don't say to. >> night	Say below. Now say below but don't say be. >> low	Say forgive. Now say forgive but don't say for >> give	Say forgot. Now say forgot but don't say for. >> got	Say belong. Now say belong but don't say be. >> long	Say anyone. Now say anyone but don't say any. >> one	Say without. Now say without but don't say with. >> out
Say tadpole. Now say tadpole but don't say tad. >> pole	Say doorstep. Now say doorstep but don't say door. >> step	Say leapfrog. Now say leapfrog but don't say leap. >> frog	Say textbook. Now say textbook but don't say text. >> book	Say passport. Now say passport but don't say pass. >> port	Say midnight. Now say midnight but don't say mid. >> night	Say outlook. Now say outlook but don't say out. >> look	Say playpen. Now say playpen but don't say play. >> pen
Say highway. Now say highway but don't say high. >> way	Say blindfold. Now say blindfold but don't say blind. >> fold	Say nickname. Now say nickname but don't say nick. >> name	Say homemade. Now say homemade but don't say home. >> made	Say greenhouse. Now say greenhouse but don't say green. >> house	Say snowman. Now say snowman but don't say snow >> man	Say earthquake. Now say earthquake but don't say earth. >> quake	Say windmill. Now say windmill but don't say wind. >> mill

Compound Words: Delete Second Word

Say outlet. Now say outlet but don't say let >> out.	Say seafood. Now say seafood but don't say food >> sea.	Say zigzag. Now say zigzag but don't say zag >> zig.	Say outfit. Now say outfit but don't say fit >> out.	Say useful. Now say useful but don't say ful >> use.	Say padlock. Now say padlock but don't say lock >> pad.	Say sawmill. Now say sawmill but don't say mill >> saw.	Say subway. Now say subway but don't say way >> sub.
Say nightmare. Now say nightmare but don't say mare >> night.	Say surfboard. Now say surfboard but don't say board >> surf.	Say gateway. Now say gateway but don't say way >> gate.	Say sunlight. Now say sunlight but don't say light >> sun.	Say soybean. Now say soybean but don't say bean >> soy.	Say roadside. Now say roadside but don't say side >> road.	Say bluebird. Now say bluebird but don't say bird >> blue.	Say courtyard. Now say courtyard but don't say yard >> court.
Say seaweed. Now say seaweed but don't say weed >> sea.	Say crossroad. Now say crossroad but don't say road >> cross.	Say worldwide. Now say worldwide but don't say wide >> world.	Say vineyard. Now say vineyard but don't say yard >> vine.	Say shipyard. Now say shipyard but don't say yard >> ship.	Say limestone. Now say limestone but don't say stone >> lime.	Say nowhere. Now say nowhere but don't say where >> no.	Say somewhere. Now say somewhere but don't say where >> some.
Say lifetime. Now say lifetime but don't say time >> life.	Say outrun. Now say outrun but don't say run >> out.	Say thereby. Now say thereby but don't say by >> there.	Say jackpot. Now say jackpot but don't say pot >> jack.	Say rosebud. Now say rosebud but don't say bud >> rose.	Say eggplant. Now say eggplant but don't say plant >> egg.	Say rainbow. Now say rainbow but don't say bow >> rain.	Say yourself. Now say yourself but don't say self >> your.
Say sometime. Now say sometime but don't say time >> some.	Say drawback. Now say drawback but don't say back >> draw.	Say shortstop. Now say shortstop but don't say stop >> short.	Say safeguard. Now say safeguard but don't say guard >> safe.	Say stockyard. Now say stockyard but don't say yard >> stock.	Say household. Now say household but don't say hold >> house.	Say northeast. Now say northeast but don't say east >> north.	Say lighthouse. Now say lighthouse but don't say house >> light.
Say dashboard. Now say dashboard but don't say board >> dash.	Say headphone. Now say headphone but don't say phone >> head.	Say quicksand. Now say quicksand but don't say sand >> quick.	Say woodworking. Now say woodworking but don't say working. >> wood.	Say driftwood. Now say driftwood but don't say wood >> drift.	Say songbird. Now say songbird but don't say bird >> song.	Say whitewash. Now say whitewash but don't say wash >> white.	Say woodwork. Now say woodwork but don't say work >> wood.

Compound Words: Delete Second Word

Say leapfrog. Now say leapfrog but don't say frog >> leap.	Say teenage. Now say teenage but don't say age >> teen.	Say footstep. Now say footstep but don't say step >> foot.	Say inside. Now say inside but don't say side >> in.	Say without. Now say without but don't say out >> with.	Say takeoff. Now say takeoff but don't say off >> take.	Say password. Now say password but don't say word >> pass.	Say hallway. Now say hallway but don't say way >> hall.
Say washtub. Now say washtub but don't say tub >> wash.	Say nineteen. Now say nineteen but don't say teen >> nine.	Say daydream. Now say daydream but don't say dream >> day.	Say headline. Now say headline but don't say line >> head.	Say horseback. Now say horseback but don't say back >> horse.	Say locksmith. Now say locksmith but don't say smith >> lock.	Say backbone. Now say backbone but don't say bone >> back.	Say southwest. Now say southwest but don't say west >> south.
Say whirlpool. Now say whirlpool but don't say pool >> whirl.	Say soundproof. Now say soundproof but don't say proof >> sound.	Say airmail. Now say airmail but don't say mail >> air.	Say watchdog. Now say watchdog but don't say dog >> watch.	Say toothpick. Now say toothpick but don't say pick >> tooth.	Say lifeboat. Now say lifeboat but don't say boat >> life.	Say pinpoint. Now say pinpoint but don't say point >> pin.	Say haystack. Now say haystack but don't say stack >> hay.
Say rainfall. Now say rainfall but don't say fall >> rain.	Say jigsaw. Now say jigsaw but don't say saw >> jig.	Say archway. Now say archway but don't say way >> arch.	Say notebook. Now say notebook but don't say book >> note.	Say suitcase. Now say suitcase but don't say case >> suit.	Say workshop. Now say workshop but don't say shop >> work.	Say eyelash. Now say eyelash but don't say lash >> eye.	Say sunburn. Now say sunburn but don't say burn >> sun.
Say backboard. Now say backboard but don't say board >> back.	Say afternoon. Now say afternoon but don't say noon >> after.	Say barefoot. Now say barefoot but don't say foot >> bare.	Say graveyard. Now say graveyard but don't say yard >> grave.	Say grandson. Now say grandson but don't say son >> grand.	Say bookcase. Now say bookcase but don't say case >> book.	Say iceberg. Now say iceberg but don't say berg >> ice.	Say gumdrop. Now say gumdrop but don't say drop >> gum.
Say countdown. Now say countdown but don't say down >> count.	Say downtown. Now say downtown but don't say town >> down.	Say pocketbook. Now say pocketbook but don't say book >> pocket.	Say springboard. Now say springboard but don't say board >> spring.	Say chessboard. Now say chessboard but don't say board >> chess.	Say homeland. Now say homeland but don't say land >> home.	Say skateboard. Now say skateboard but don't say board >> skate.	Say nightfall. Now say nightfall but don't say fall >> night.

Say near. Now say near but don't say /n/. >> ear.	Say pies. Now say pies but don't say /p/. >> eyes.	Say leg. Now say leg but don't say /l/. >> egg.	Say pod. Now say pod but don't say /p/. >> odd.	Say fear. Now say fear but don't say /f/. >> ear.	Say thus. Now say thus but don't say /th/. >> us.	Say nod. Now say nod but don't say /n/. >> odd.	Say fuse. Now say fuse but don't say /f/. >> use.
Say there. Now say there but don't say /th/. >> air.	Say peach. Now say peach but don't say /p/. >> each.	Say same. Now say same but don't say /s/. >> aim.	Say wear. Now say wear but don't say /w/. >> air.	Say name. Now say name but don't say /n/. >> aim.	Say more. Now say more but don't say /m/. >> or.	Say guide. Now say guide but don't say /g/. >> I'd.	Say ledge. Now say ledge but don't say /l/. >> edge.
Say gill. Now say gill but don't say /g/. >> ill.	Say fin. Now say fin but don't say /f/. >> in.	Say for. Now say for but don't say /f/. >> or.	Say his. Now say his but don't say /h/. >> is.	Say lit. Now say lit but don't say /l/. >> it.	Say mill. Now say mill but don't say /m/. >> ill.	Say soar. Now say soar but don't say /s/. >> oar.	Say foil. Now say foil but don't say /f/. >> oil.
Say peel. Now say peel but don't say /p/. >> eel.	Say gear. Now say gear but don't say /g/. >> ear.	Say ride. Now say ride but don't say /r/. >> I'd.	Say rice. Now say rice but don't say /r/. >> ice.	Say win. Now say win but don't say /w/. >> in.	Say late. Now say late but don't say /l/. >> ate.	Say lace. Now say lace but don't say /l/. >> ace.	Say knit. Now say knit but don't say /kn/. >> it.
Say sad. Now say sad but don't say /s/. >> add.	Say thin. Now say thin but don't say /th/. >> in.	Say rich. Now say rich but don't say /r/. >> itch.	Say head. Now say head but don't say /h/. >> Ed.	Say care. Now say care but don't say /c/. >> air.	Say lake. Now say lake but don't say /l/. >> ache.	Say had. Now say had but don't say /h/. >> add.	Say pear. Now say pear but don't say /p/. >> air.
Say feet. Now say feet but don't say /f/. >> eat.	Say heat. Now say heat but don't say /h/. >> eat.	Say cash. Now say cash but don't say /c/. >> ash.	Say fox. Now say fox but don't say /f/. >> ox.	Say shin. Now say shin but don't say /sh/. >> in.	Say goat. Now say goat but don't say /g/. >> oat.	Say cape. Now say cape but don't say /c/. >> ape.	Say pace. Now say pace but don't say /p/. >> ace.

Delete Beginning Sound

Say nose. Now say nose but don't say /n/. >> owes.	Say rose. Now say rose but don't say /r/. >> owes.	Say where. Now say where but don't say /w/. >> air.	Say whale. Now say whale but don't say /wh/. >> ale.	Say shove. Now say shove but don't say /sh/. >> of.	Say chime. Now say chime but don't say /ch/. >> I'm.	Say door. Now say door but don't say /d/. >> or.	Say dime. Now say dime but don't say /d/. >> I'm.
Say face. Now say face but don't say /f/. >> ace.	Say love. Now say love but don't say /l/. >> of.	Say fair. Now say fair but don't say /f/. >> air.	Say lash. Now say lash but don't say /l/. >> ash.	Say cat. Now say cat but don't say /c/. >> at.	Say four. Now say four but don't say /f/. >> or.	Say hair. Now say hair but don't say /h/. >> air.	Say pour. Now say pour but don't say /p/. >> or.
Say lone. Now say lone but don't say /l/. >> own.	Say paid. Now say paid but don't say /p/. >> aid.	Say fall. Now say fall but don't say /f/. >> all.	Say rate. Now say rate but don't say /r/. >> ate.	Say hear. Now say hear but don't say /h/. >> ear.	Say wall. Now say wall but don't say /w/. >> all.	Say hat. Now say hat but don't say /h/. >> at.	Say mitt. Now say mitt but don't say /m/. >> it.
Say gate. Now say gate but don't say /g/. >> ate.	Say five. Now say five but don't say /f/. >> I've.	Say dial. Now say dial but don't say /d/. >> aisle.	Say sour. Now say sour but don't say /s/. >> our.	Say tar. Now say tar but don't say /t/. >> are.	Say that. Now say that but don't say /th/. >> at.	Say rake. Now say rake but don't say /r/. >> ache.	Say coat. Now say coat but don't say /c/. >> oat.
Say leaves. Now say leaves but don't say /l/. >> eves.	Say shape. Now say shape but don't say /sh/. >> ape.	Say rhyme. Now say rhyme but don't say /rh/. >> I'm.	Say fame. Now say fame but don't say /f/. >> aim.	Say pants. Now say pants but don't say /p/. >> ants.	Say sown. Now say sown but don't say /s/. >> own.	Say shade. Now say shade but don't say /sh/. >> ade.	Say deer. Now say deer but don't say /d/. >> ear.
Say goes. Now say goes but don't say /g/. >> owes.	Say pouch. Now say pouch but don't say /p/. >> ouch.	Say weight. Now say weight but don't say /wh/. >> ate.	Say candy. Now say candy but don't say /can/. >> dy.	Say cheese. Now say cheese but don't say /ch/. >> ease.	Say known. Now say known but don't say /kn/. >> own.	Say hedge. Now say hedge but don't say /h/. >> edge.	Say wheel. Now say wheel but don't say /wh/. >> eel.

Delete Final Sound

Say and. Now say and but don't say /d/.>> an.	Say bend. Now say bend but don't say /d/.>> been.	Say art. Now say art but don't say /t/.>> are.	Say card. Now say card but don't say /d/.>> car.	Say inch. Now say inch but don't say /ch/.>> in.	Say farm. Now say farm but don't say /m/.>> far.	Say cold. Now say cold but don't say /d/.>> coal.	Say firm. Now say firm but don't say /m/.>> fur.
Say cart. Now say cart but don't say /t/.>> car.	Say hats. Now say hats but don't say /s/.>> hat.	Say arc. Now say arc but don't say /k/.>> are.	Say felt. Now say felt but don't say /t/.>> fell.	Say eyes. Now say eyes but don't say /z/.>> eye.	Say force. Now say force but don't say /s/.>> for.	Say arm. Now say arm but don't say /m/.>> are.	Say grasp. Now say grasp but don't say /p/.>> grass.
Say toes. Now say toes but don't say /s/.>> toe.	Say self. Now say self but don't say /f/.>> sell.	Say ant. Now say ant but don't say /t/.>> an.	Say band. Now say band but don't say /d/.>> ban.	Say false. Now say false but don't say /s/.>> fall.	Say barn. Now say barn but don't say /n/.>> bar.	Say mist. Now say mist but don't say /t/.>> miss.	Say fork. Now say fork but don't say /k/.>> for.
Say lost. Now say lost but don't say /t/.>> loss.	Say cats. Now say cats but don't say /s/.>> cat.	Say herd. Now say herd but don't say /d/.>> her.	Say clamp. Now say clamp but don't say /p/.>> clam.	Say shelf. Now say shelf but don't say /f/.>> shell.	Say cord. Now say cord but don't say /d/.>> core.	Say dent. Now say dent but don't say /t/.>> den.	Say gold. Now say gold but don't say /d/.>> goal.
Say surf. Now say surf but don't say /f/.>> sir.	Say bolt. Now say bolt but don't say /t/.>> bowl.	Say fault. Now say fault but don't say /t/.>> fall.	Say slump. Now say slump but don't say /p/.>> slum.	Say guilt. Now say guilt but don't say /t/.>> gill.	Say belt. Now say belt but don't say /t/.>> bell.	Say tend. Now say tend but don't say /d/.>> ten.	Say dense. Now say dense but don't say /s/.>> den.
Say worm. Now say worm but don't say /m/.>> were.	Say sword. Now say sword but don't say /d/.>> sore.	Say bold. Now say bold but don't say /d/.>> bowl.	Say worn. Now say worn but don't say /n/.>> wore.	Say storm. Now say storm but don't say /m/.>> store.	Say porch. Now say porch but don't say /ch/.>> poor.	Say dorm. Now say dorm but don't say /m/.>> door.	Say stork. Now say stork but don't say /k/.>> store.

Reading Remediation Pathway: Levels 1-5

Delete Final Sound

Say bask. Now say bask but don't say /k/.>> bass.	Say mild. Now say mild but don't say /d/.>> mile.	Say yelp. Now say yelp but don't say /p/.>> yell.	Say past. Now say past but don't say /t/.>> pass.	Say halt. Now say halt but don't say /t/.>> hall.	Say park. Now say park but don't say /k/.>> par.	Say paste. Now say paste but don't say /t/.>> pace.	Say build. Now say build but don't say /d/.>> bill.
Say plant. Now say plant but don't say /t/.>> plan.	Say course. Now say course but don't say /s/.>> core.	Say pinch. Now say pinch but don't say /ch/.>> pin.	Say baste. Now say baste but don't say /t/.>> base.	Say mold. Now say mold but don't say /d/.>> mole.	Say sort. Now say sort but don't say /t/.>> sore.	Say search. Now say search but don't say /ch/.>> sir.	Say meant. Now say meant but don't say /t/.>> men.
Say heard. Now say heard but don't say /d/.>> her.	Say stark. Now say stark but don't say /k/.>> star.	Say dealt. Now say dealt but don't say /t/.>> dell.	Say sold. Now say sold but don't say /d/.>> sole.	Say weld. Now say weld but don't say /d/.>> well.	Say fort. Now say fort but don't say /t/.>> for.	Say tenth. Now say tenth but don't say /th/.>> ten.	Say bald. Now say bald but don't say /d/.>> ball.
Say lined. Now say lined but don't say /d/.>> line.	Say tarp. Now say tarp but don't say /p/.>> tar.	Say brand. Now say brand but don't say /d/.>> bran.	Say fourth. Now say fourth but don't say /th/.>> four.	Say word. Now say word but don't say /d/.>> were.	Say bird. Now say bird but don't say /d/.>> burr.	Say hilt. Now say hilt but don't say /t/.>> hill.	Say guest. Now say guest but don't say /t/.>> guess.
Say yelp. Now say yelp but don't say /p/.>> yell.	Say hold. Now say hold but don't say /d/.>> hole.	Say rink. Now say rink but don't say /k/.>> ring.	Say film. Now say film but don't say /m/.>> fill.	Say clasp. Now say clasp but don't say /p/.>> class.	Say lamp. Now say lamp but don't say /p/.>> lamb.	Say once. Now say once but don't say /s/.>> one.	Say paint. Now say paint but don't say /t/.>> pain.
Say find. Now say find but don't say /d/.>> fine.	Say tarp. Now say tarp but don't say /p/.>> tar.	Say pence. Now say pence but don't say /s/.>> pen.	Say stork. Now say stork but don't say /k/.>> store.	Say Gramp. Now say Gramp but don't say /p/.>> gram.	Say York. Now say York but don't say /k/.>> your.	Say worst. Now say worst but don't say /t/.>> worse.	Say launch. Now say launch but don't say /ch/.>> lawn.

Made in the USA
Columbia, SC
07 August 2021